Alabama

Alabama

Lucile Davis

Children's Press®
A Division of Grolier Publishing
New York London Hong Kong Sydney
Danbury, Connecticut

Frontispiece: Japanese Gardens, Mobile, Alabama
Front cover: Bellingrath Gardens
Back cover: The Alabama state capitol

Consultant: Rubye Sullivan, Alabama State University

Please note: All statistics are as up-to-date as possible at the time of publication.

Visit Children's Press on the Internet at http://publishing.grolier.com

Book production by Editorial Directions, Inc.

Library of Congress Cataloging-in-Publication Data

Davis, Lucile.
    Alabama / Lucile Davis.
        p. cm. — (America the beautiful. Second series)
    Includes bibliographical references and index.
    Summary : Describes the geography, plants, animals, history, economy, language,
religions, culture, sports, art, and people of this southern state, whose first European
settlers were Spanish and French rather than British.
    ISBN 0-516-20683-4
    1. Alabama—Juvenile literature. [1. Alabama.] I. Title. II. Series.
F326.3.D38 1999
976.1—dc21   98-19621
                                                                                    CIP
                                                                                    AC

Acknowledgments

Thanks to the friendly, helpful folks who work for the Alabama state government. A special thanks to the people in the Governor's Office, particularly John Mark and Odessia Ayers. For their help, suggestions, and support, a big "thank y'all" to the LLLoop, my virtual watercooler crowd. A "cum laude" thank you to Linda and Chuck George for help and support above and beyond. And last, but most important, I owe more than is printable to my parents for their lifetime of support.

Rosa Parks

Commercial fishing boat

DeSoto State Park

Contents

Nineteenth-century
plantation owner

Gray fox

Northwestern
Alabama

Modern Choctaw
dancer

A rocket in
Huntsville

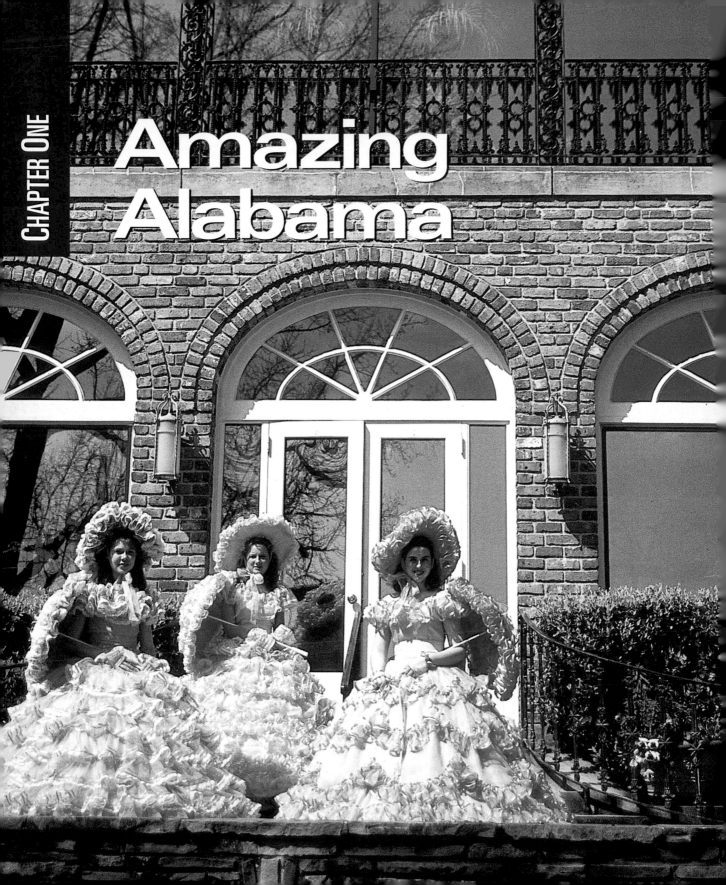

CHAPTER ONE

Amazing Alabama

A young woman smoothes down the layered ruffles on the long, bell-shaped skirt of her lavender dress, then adjusts her wide-brimmed hat with lavender ribbons. Her clothes are perfect for a summer day in Alabama's pre–Civil War period. She takes a last look at her costume before heading downstairs to meet the people she will take on a guided tour of Bellingrath Gardens just south of Mobile. She will spend her summer taking

The Oakleigh Mansion in Mobile receives hundreds of visitors each year.

visitors on a trip back in time to discover what Alabama was like more than 100 years ago.

At Huntsville, in the northern part of the state, a young man in an orange flight suit sits in a mock-up of the space shuttle's command module and explains takeoff and landing procedures to his audience. Later, he will show these "Space Campers" how it feels to be weightless. The young man works for the National Aeronautic and Space Administration (NASA) in Huntsville. He will spend his summer showing people how Alabama is helping NASA prepare for future space missions.

What a different summer these two young people will have! She will spend her time talking about the past. He will spend his

Opposite: Young women dressed as Southern belles at Bellingrath Gardens

time talking about the future. Their summer jobs are so different, so diverse—very much like their home state of Alabama.

This is Alabama—a state of surprises, unique places and people, and a friendly atmosphere as warm and inviting as its climate. The state is steeped in history, reaching back to a time when explorers first came to the North American continent. As it reaches into the future, the state offers schools, businesses, and industries the opportunity for research through state-of-the-art "supercomputing."

Unique places can be found all over the state. There are mountains to climb and caves to explore. In some places, scientists are still able to find new species of plant and animal life. A huge onyx cave that was a campsite for prehistoric people is now the site of a sound and laser-light show. Alabama also has a major shipping and fishing port, where the fish seem so eager to be caught they actually jump onto the beach.

Alabama has the largest native-born population in the United States—which means folks who were born in the state, known as the Heart of Dixie, prefer to stay there. Its famous people include heroes and leaders of the civil rights movement of the 1960s, sports Hall-of-Famers, popular entertainers, music legends, and nationally recognized politicians and business people.

Nature has also blessed Alabama. A mild climate and rich soil make for good farming. Ore and mineral deposits in the northern part of the state feed the steel industry. Alabama's marble rivals Italy's for texture and hardness. The longest natural rock bridge in the eastern United States and the deepest gorge east of the Mississippi River are both found in Alabama. Forests cover two-thirds of the state and are complemented by many rivers and man-made lakes. The forests and waterways provide year-round recreational activities, which include camping, hiking, boating, hunting, fishing, and spelunking.

Spelunking is the activity of exploring caves. The caves of Alabama reveal the state's earliest history. Signs of prehistoric man are still evident there for all to see. The story of the caves, then, is a good place to start the story of Alabama.

Geopolitical map of Alabama

CHAPTER TWO

Early Times, Early Settlers

Russell Cave in Bridgeport

Humans have lived in Alabama for about 10,000 years. In 1957, in a cave in northeast Alabama, a team of scientists discovered the oldest set of human remains found in North America. Along with the human bones, the scientists found tools and weapons. From these discoveries and with the help of carbon dating—a method of determining the age of prehistoric material—the scientists were able to piece together information about these early Alabamians. They were a nomadic people, moving from place to place as they followed the animals they hunted for food. They also gathered and ate berries and roots. The caves were used as shelter and bases from which to hunt.

By 1,000 B.C., the nomadic people began to plant crops and develop better tools. They lived in tribes—groups related through common ancestors, customs, and laws. These tribes gathered into villages, where they built lodges around large mounds that were as high as 60 feet (18 m). The mounds were the centers of the village's religious and cultural life. Often temples or the homes of tribal leaders were built on top of these mounds. Sometimes, the mounds were also sacred burial places. The mound-builder society, known as the Mississippian Culture, existed between A.D. 800 and 1500.

Opposite: Modern Choctaw dancers pose for a photographer at the Moundville's Native American Festival.

Russell Cave National Monument Park

According to evidence that archaeologists have found by digging through layers of soil, humans were living in Russell Cave more than 9,000 years ago. The early inhabitants were nomads who hunted large animals—their main source of food—with chipped rocks and notched bones as weapons. A second layer of evidence shows that later inhabitants were family groups that made the cave their permanent home. These people made tools and pottery, and may have traded with other people in other regions. Later, a third group of people used the cave primarily as a winter hunting shelter.

Today, Russell Cave is a national monument, run by the National Park Service. Its archaeological evidence of Alabama's early people is on display in sections of the cave and at the Visitor Center and Museum. The park also offers primitive tool demonstrations and educational programs. There are walking trails around the cave that provide a look at the natural living conditions of the inhabitants. Russell Cave National Monument Park is located 7 miles (11 km) north of Bridgeport, Alabama. ■

Their villages extended from what is now the state of Illinois to the Gulf of Mexico.

In the early seventeenth century, the mound-builder society disappeared, although scientists are still puzzled as to why and how. After the mound builders disappeared, a new group of native peoples began settling in the lands that are now Alabama. Scientists believe that these people were descended from the mound builders.

They lived in tribes and spoke a language known as Muskogean. Because of a common language and common interests, these tribes formed a loosely knit union that became known as the Creek Confederacy.

Touring Moundville

One of the largest mound villages in North America is located in Moundville on the Black Warrior River in west central Alabama. This village was a trade and cultural center for about 10,000 people of the Mississippian Culture living in the area during the twelfth and thirteenth centuries. The Moundville community had a population of more than 1,000 people. By 1350, the once-prosperous community began to lose its importance. The people disappeared. No one really knows where they went. They did, however, leave evidence of their existence in and around the mounds.

Moundville Archaeological Park, located south of Tuscaloosa, provides a close look at this prehistoric mound culture. The Edward T. Douglass Nature Trail extends through 0.5 miles (0.8 km) of woodlands. The boardwalk trail winds past several of the mounds and takes visitors from ground level to treetop height for a look at how early peoples lived. The Jones Archaeological Museum exhibits bones, tools, jewelry, weapons, and other interesting objects found in and around the mounds. Each September, the park hosts the Moundville Native American Festival. ■

The word *Alabama* comes from the name of one of the Creek tribes—the Alibamu. *Alibamu* means "I open [clear] the thicket" and refers to the tribe's practice of clearing land for planting crops. Other Muskogean-speaking people were the Chickasaw and the Choctaw. The last native group to arrive in Alabama before European settlement began were the Cherokee, whose language was Iroquois. They moved to Alabama from Georgia to escape the European settlers.

An outside view of the reconstructed mound-builder village at Moundville

The Search for Gold

Alabama was first explored and colonized by the Spanish and the French. When he sailed into Mobile Bay in 1519, Alonso Álvarez de Piñeda was the first Spaniard to see the land that is now Alabama. In 1540, the Spanish explorer Hernando de Soto landed in Florida searching for land and gold. He found lots of desirable land, but little gold. In his quest for riches, de Soto became an unwelcome visitor to Native American villages. He took food, horses, and other goods to supply his troops

Hernando de Soto brought soldiers and Catholic missionaries to the Americas.

Hernando de Soto

Hernando de Soto was born in one of the last years of the fifteenth century in southwestern Spain. His first trip to the Americas was with Pedrarias Davila to explore Central America. He participated in the conquest of Nicaragua and Peru. Later he was appointed governor of Cuba. In 1539, under a grant from the King of Spain, de Soto began an exploration of North America. De Soto was searching for gold. His travels took him through the southern states and ended on the banks of the Mississippi. There, de Soto caught a fever and died on May 21, 1542. ■

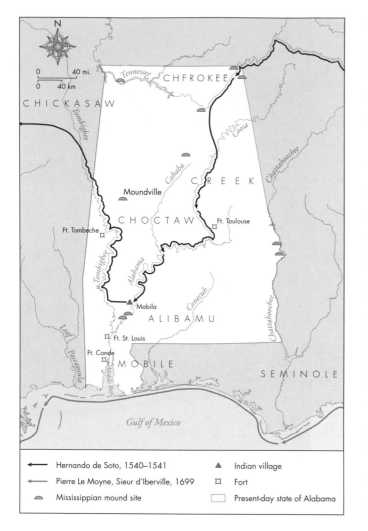

0 — 40 mi.
0 — 40 km

CHEROKEE
CHICKASAW
CREEK
Moundville
CHOCTAW   Ft. Toulouse
Ft. Tombeche
Mabila
ALIBAMU
Ft. St. Louis
Ft. Conde
MOBILE
SEMINOLE

Tennessee
Tombigbee
Coosa
Cahaba
Chattahoochee
Tombigbee
Alabama
Conecuh
Chattahoochee
Leaf
Pascagoula
Mobile Bay

Gulf of Mexico

⟵— Hernando de Soto, 1540–1541   ▲ Indian village
⟵— Pierre Le Moyne, Sieur d'Iberville, 1699   ⌑ Fort
◠ Mississippian mound site   ▢ Present-day state of Alabama

Exploration of Alabama

and enslaved the natives to carry his supplies. He often killed or tortured natives who refused to comply with his demands or provide information about where to find gold.

One of the native leaders, Chief Tuscaloosa, which means "Black Warrior," knew about de Soto's bloody reputation. He also knew de Soto was on his way toward Mabila in the southwestern region where Tuscalusa's people lived. The chief ordered all the fields cleared to keep de Soto from finding food. The chief prepared his people to fight, but it was a lost cause—the Spaniards had guns. Thousands of Tuscaloosa's people died, including, it is believed, Chief Tuscaloosa. The Black Warrior River is named for this chief, who was said to stand more than 7 feet (2.1 m) tall.

Tuscaloosa's people may have lost the fight, but they won the war. The battle exhausted the Spaniards and wounded many. De Soto and his men fled Alabama.

In 1559, the Spanish tried to start a colony near Mobile Bay. Tristán de Luna and 1,000 colonists were sent to search for the gold that de Soto had never found. Unsuccessful, the Spanish abandoned the area three years later.

French Settlement

The French also tried to settle Alabama. In 1689, René-Robert Cavelier, Sieur de La Salle, took a trip down the Mississippi to the Gulf of Mexico. He claimed all the land drained by the river for France. Although the exact boundaries are not known, the claim is believed to have included the land that is now Alabama. This large tract, named for France's king, Louis XIV, is known as the Louisiana Territory.

The French were the first to successfully establish a permanent group of white settlers in the region of Alabama. Louis XIV sent Pierre Le Moyne, Sieur d'Iberville, and Jean-Baptiste Le Moyne, Sieur de Bienville, to govern the Louisiana Territory. The brothers landed on Dauphin Island in Mobile Bay in 1699. In 1702, they established the territorial capital at a site on a bluff near the Mobile River. They named it Fort Louis de la Mobile. In 1711, a flood washed away Fort Louis, and the brothers moved the capital to the site of present-day Mobile. This capital was also named Fort Louis, but was renamed Fort Conde de la Mobile in 1720.

France established a colony close to Fort Louis, which came to be known as Mobile. The purpose of this colony was to produce commercial crops of sugar, rice, and indigo (a plant that produces a blue dye). To help harvest these crops, the French enslaved 600 Africans and transported them to the colony in 1719. This action marked the beginning of two and a half centuries of slavery in the American South. France gave the colonists very little additional support, however. At times, the people nearly starved waiting for supply ships from home. In 1720, the territorial capital was moved to New Biloxi, and in 1722, to New Orleans.

French fur traders trapped beaver and fur-bearing animals along Alabama's numerous lakes and rivers.

France had dominated the fur trade until the early eighteenth century, when Great Britain became a competitor. Growing trade and settlement competitions between the British and French led to the French and Indian War (1754–1763). Under the terms of the Treaty of Paris, signed in 1763, the defeated French gave up their lands west of the Mississippi River to Spain and their lands east of the river—including present-day Alabama—to Great Britain.

Struggles to Statehood

The British governed Alabama for only seventeen years before the American Revolution began. The 1783 treaty ending the war made the Mississippi River the western boundary of the United States of America. Northern Alabama was included in the lands that the British gave to the United States. Mobile and other parts of southern Alabama were still ruled by Spain, however.

In 1800, France forced Spain to give up its claims to the land. Then, in 1803, France sold the entire Louisiana Territory to the United States in an exchange known as the Louisiana Purchase. Although the United States believed that the Mobile region was included in the purchase, Spain still considered it part of Florida, which was under Spanish rule.

In the early nineteenth century, the United States and Britain were again quarreling over trade and territory. In 1812, the quarrel became a fight. The Indians, who resisted further U.S. set-

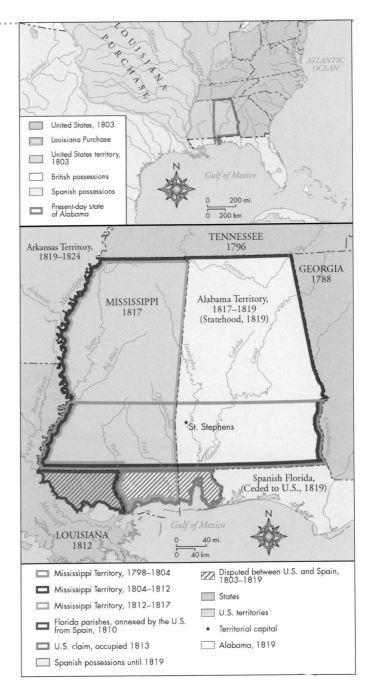

Historical map of Alabama

In the War of 1812, many American Indians joined the British forces against General Andrew Jackson's troops.

tlement of their lands, were allied with the British. In 1813, Creek Indians raided Fort Mims a few miles north of Mobile, killing hundreds of settlers. General Andrew Jackson led his Tennessee militia against the Creek, winning battles at Talladega and Horseshoe Bend. When the War of 1812 ended in 1814, the strong Creek Confederacy had been broken. Jackson's victories in Alabama made

The New State

In 1819, the first state constitutional convention assembled in the town of Huntsville in northern Alabama Territory. After Alabama became the twenty-second state on December 14, 1819, Huntsville served as the state capital for a little more than one year.

A Georgia physician, William Wyatt Bibb, had been the governor of Alabama Territory. In 1819, he became the first governor of the state. Bibb helped form the government and pass the laws for the new state. The state's first U.S. senators were William Rufus King and John W. Walker.

The town of Cahaba, where the Cahaba and Alabama Rivers meet, became the state capital in 1820. The Alabama River flooded in 1825, causing great damage to Cahaba, and the capital was moved to Tuscaloosa in 1826. Tuscaloosa served as the state capital until 1846, when the present-day capital of Montgomery was established. ■

him popular throughout the United States, which helped him win the presidential election in 1828.

During the War of 1812, American troops won the Mobile region from the Spanish. When the war ended, the defeated Creek gave up all of their lands—a region that was almost two-thirds of present-day state Alabama. The U.S. flag was now the only flag flying over the land, and Congress declared Alabama a territory in 1817. St. Stephens, on the Tombigbee River in southwest Alabama, became the territorial capital.

Settlers rushed to Alabama Territory to claim parcels of fertile plains and forest land for farming. Two years later, the territory met the population requirements for statehood. On December 14, 1819, Alabama became the twenty-second state in the union.

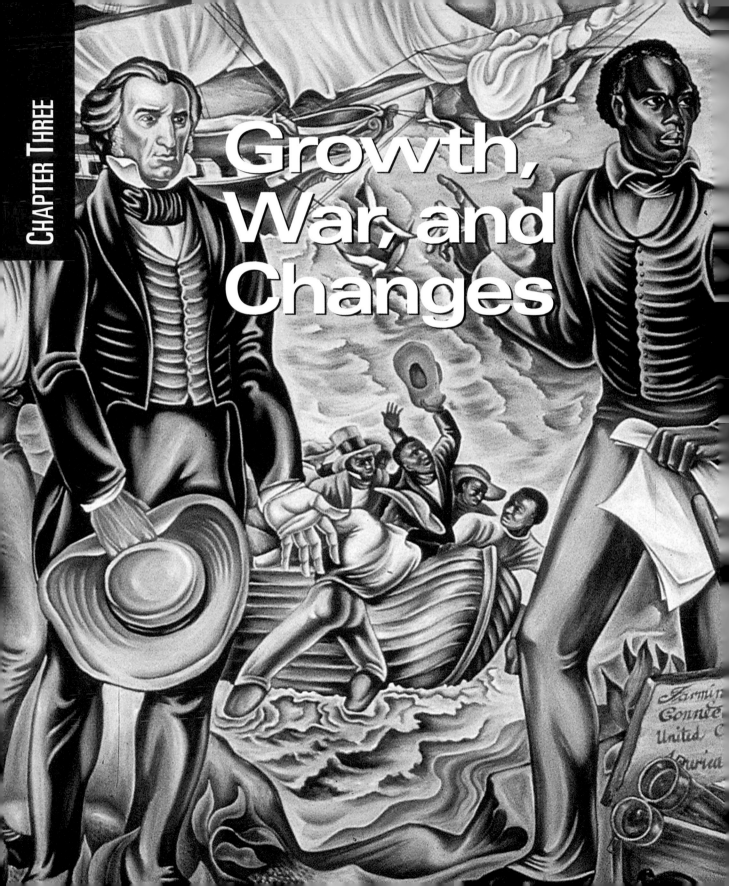

CHAPTER THREE

Growth, War, and Changes

In the ten years after Alabama became a state, settlers continued to pour in, and the state's population doubled. The state's slave population kept pace. Cotton had become the most important crop and the basis for the state's economic stability. Growing and picking cotton required a large workforce, and plantation owners bought enslaved Africans to provide the labor. The state population numbers nearly doubled again from 1830 to 1840.

By the beginning of the Civil War in 1861, Alabama's slave population almost equaled the white population. Because the state economy depended on cotton and the slave labor required to produce it, plantation owners rejected any attempts to abolish slavery. Northern states in the United States began to call for an end to slavery, placing them in direct conflict with the South, which had become dependent on slave labor. The history of Alabama in the nineteenth century is the story of this conflict and its aftermath.

A hand-colored woodcut portraying the picking, bailing, and ginning of cotton

Growth, Industry, and Commerce

The new state grew quickly. Steamboats began to travel up and down the state waterways delivering people, building and household goods, and commercial products. Land companies promoted

Opposite: A mural showing slave uprisings in the 1840s

Alabama's Growing Population

Year	White	Slave	Total**
1820	85,000	42,000	128,000
1830*	190,406	117,549	309,527
1840	335,185	253,532	590,756
1850	426,514	342,844	771,623
1860	526,271	435,080	964,201

* First year U.S. Census figures available.

**Free-black population numbers are not listed, therefore the combined White and Slave totals do not equal the Total population figure. ■

the sale of property in the state, and many people of wealth and influence moved to Alabama. The first smelters—which melt iron ore to produce metal—near Russellville were laying the foundation for what would become a huge iron and steel industry.

The state also had a large slave labor force, rich soil in the central Black Belt of the state, and waterway transportation to the Gulf. Because of these factors and advantages—and the invention of Eli Whitney's cotton gin—Alabama's cotton plantations were producing large quantities of cotton for sale throughout the United States and Europe. Cotton had become the most important crop in the state.

Eli Whitney's Cotton Gin

In 1792, Eli Whitney attended a dinner party. Guests were discussing the reasons why growing cotton was becoming unprofitable. Even using slaves, they said, too much time was required to separate by hand the seeds from the cotton fibers. One person took a full day to separate the seeds from 1 pound (.45 kg) of cotton. Whitney was a skilled mechanic, and the guests suggested he solve the problem.

By April of the next year, Whitney had designed a machine that enabled one man to produce 50 pounds (23 kg) of clean cotton a day. With this efficient machine, cotton growing and processing again became profitable. Because of Whitney's innovative machine, the United States soon became the largest producer of cotton in the world. ■

The Issue of Slavery

By the middle of the nineteenth century, slavery was becoming a heated issue in the United States. It was an economic issue as well as a moral one. Many people in the United States had always been opposed to slavery—in fact, the issue had been debated by the framers and signers of the Constitution. Slavery had survived, however, because of its economic importance.

Loading cotton onto a steamboat

By the mid-1800s, the North was no longer economically dependent on slavery. This enabled those Northerners who had always opposed the practice to start actively opposing slavery on moral grounds. Many people in Alabama were also opposed to slavery. Two-thirds of the state's white population did not own slaves. The entire Alabama economy, however, had grown dependent on cotton production, which relied on slave labor. Most people could not afford to oppose slavery.

Congress had also passed protective tariffs on certain goods manufactured in the North, which made these needed goods very expensive in the South. Because of these tariffs and the North's demand that the South free its slaves, many Southerners felt that the North was interfering with their business. They believed that each

Trails of Tears

The rapid population growth in Alabama during its early years of statehood created a demand for more land. To meet this demand throughout the Southeast, the U.S. government acquired Native American lands through treaties favoring the white settlers. The Choctaw gave up their land in the 1830 treaty of Dancing Rabbit Creek. The entire tribe gathered near Livingston for three days of mourning and crying before they left their ancestral lands and headed for Indian Territory (now the state of Oklahoma).

The Chickasaw gave up their land and moved west in 1832. The Creek were also forced to sign a treaty that year. Some of them went south to Florida, however, where Alabama native Osceola led a Seminole Indian revolt. An appeal from both state governors convinced the Creeks to keep the peace. The Creeks and the Seminoles eventually moved to Indian Territory.

The Cherokee refused to sign a treaty. In 1838, federal troops marched into their lands, part of which was the remaining Native American territory in northern Alabama. The troops removed the Cherokee from their lands in a forced march that became known as the Trail of Tears.

The Cherokee were driven in front of bayonets at a fast pace. Those who could not keep up were beaten. Many thousands died. One Cherokee man later told a historian of the sadness of his people. White settlers, who watched the long lines of Native Americans march to Indian Territory, wrote to their relatives of the pity they felt for these people and the tragedy of the many deaths. One soldier assigned to the march wrote that it was the cruelest work he ever knew. ■

state should have the right to make its own laws without interference from the federal government or other states. With their economy and their state's sovereignty threatened, people in Alabama felt they had no choice but to secede (withdraw) from the Union.

Jefferson Davis

The Confederate States of America

The Union came undone when Republican Abraham Lincoln was elected president in 1861 on an antislavery platform. Alabama seceded from the Union on January 11, 1861, and declared itself the Republic of Alabama. The new republic invited other southern states to send delegates to a convention to be held in Montgomery.

On February 8, the Confederate States of America was established. Jefferson Davis, a former cotton planter and secretary of war

William Rufus King

William Rufus King was a member of the constitutional convention that drafted Alabama's first constitution in 1819. He also became one of Alabama's first two U.S. senators. King opposed slavery and, while in Congress, he worked to settle the differences between the northern and southern states. In 1852, King was elected vice president of the United States—the highest office ever held by an Alabamian—under fellow Democrat Franklin Pierce. King, who had tuberculosis, died six weeks after taking office, but Pierce and the Democratic Party continued to seek solutions to the slavery issue. ∎

under President Franklin Pierce, was elected the confederate president. Alexander Stephens was elected vice president. Montgomery was chosen as the first capital of the new nation. Because of this status, Montgomery is called the Cradle of the Confederacy. Four months later, the Confederate Congress voted to move the capital to Richmond, Virginia. Although the move disappointed many Alabamians, it kept the state from becoming a prime battleground during the great war that was soon to begin.

The American Civil War

In April 1861, Confederate troops fired on Fort Sumter, located 6 miles (10 km) southeast of Charleston, South Carolina. This event marks the beginning of the American Civil War. An estimated 122,000 Alabamians went to war; approximately 45,000 died. About 10,000 blacks and 2,500 whites joined the Union army.

Union soldiers occupied Huntsville, Decatur, and Tuscumbia in 1862, but much of Alabama escaped destruction during the war.

Few battles were fought inside the borders of the state. One of the war's most important sea battles, however, was fought in Mobile Bay.

In 1864, Union admiral David Farragut led an eighteen-ship fleet into Mobile Bay to prevent guns and supplies from reaching the Confederate soldiers. A small fleet of Confederate warships guarded the harbor. The Union's lead ship, the USS *Tecumseh,* was hit by a torpedo shot from one of the two forts protecting the har-

Admiral Farragut rallies his troops at the Battle of Mobile Bay.

Fort Morgan

Fort Morgan was one of two Confederate forts that defended Mobile Bay during the 1864 attack by Union admiral David Farragut. The pentagon-shaped fort, constructed from 1819 to 1834, was designed by the French military engineer Simon Bernard. The fort has unique characteristics, specific to its mission of protecting a harbor rather than the fort's own location.

Fort Morgan is entered from the land side, through the hill that protects the walls of the fort from cannon fire. During the Battle of Mobile Bay, gun batteries on the harbor side were supported by a hotshot furnace. A hotshot furnace is an oven designed to heat cannon balls until they are red-hot. The red-hot balls were fired at wooden ships in the bay with the hope that the ships would catch fire. The narrow stairs leading to the batteries were designed to limit the passage of enemy soldiers if they attempted to storm the fort.

The short-barreled guns mounted in the casemates (protected enclosures) were aimed at the dry ditch that surrounds the fort. These cannons, called carronades, fired canisters (encased shots) or grapeshot (clusters of small iron balls), much like giant shotguns. ■

bor. Farragut commanded his remaining ships forward with the battle cry "Damn the torpedoes! Full speed ahead!" The Union ships took Mobile Bay, sealing it against shipping and effectively cutting off the line of supplies to the Confederates.

The Aftermath of War

The Civil War ended in 1865. Although Alabama did not suffer as much destruction as other southern states, many lives and much property were lost during the war. Areas where fighting occurred were devastated. Homes, businesses, farms, railroads, and large plantations lay in ruins. People were hungry and sick. The state and local governments were in chaos, and lawlessness made the hard times worse.

The Civil War freed Alabama's almost 500,000 slaves. These newly freed African-Americans began to look forward to having all the rights granted to citizens of the United States. A backlash against the freed slaves, however, led the Alabama legislature to pass laws that became known as the Black Codes. These codes restricted travel and work opportunities for African-Americans. Alabama also refused to ratify (approve) the Fourteenth Amendment to the Constitution, which prohibited any state from denying any citizen's legal rights—including the right to vote.

Reconstruction—the federal government's plan to restore state governments in the defeated South—led to more difficulties. In 1867, federal troops moved into Alabama, placing it under military rule. In 1868, the state ratified a new constitution that protected the civil rights of African-American citizens, and Alabama was readmitted to the United States.

Gains and Losses

From 1868 to 1874, however, the state was in political turmoil. The state government was run by Northerners who moved South after the war (known as carpetbaggers) and white Alabamians who had opposed secession (known as scalawags). As African-Americans began to exercise their rights and gain influence in government, racial tensions in the state intensified. Many people were angry, and their anger turned to violence. In the late 1860s, groups such as the Ku Klux Klan, whose members believed in white supremacy, began to terrorize and frequently kill African-Americans. In 1874, the federal government ended Reconstruction and withdrew its troops. White Democrats of Alabama, most of whom had been supporters of the Confederacy, regained political control of the state.

After the Civil War, Alabama laws restricted African-Americans from many public places.

With their rights again restricted, many African-Americans chose to remain on the plantations, working the cotton crops for wages. Others tried sharecropping. In this system, farmers worked small plots of land owned by a plantation owner. The laborers were paid a portion of the profit from the sale of their crops. Owners, however, charged the sharecroppers for food, tools, and other necessities. At the end of a growing year, most sharecroppers found that they owed money to the plantation owners. The debt was carried and grew from one year to the next, one generation to the next. The sharecropping system was almost as bad as slavery.

An Industrial Revolution

Toward the end of the nineteenth century, industry began to thrive in Alabama. These new enterprises provided African-Americans and poor whites with an alternative to sharecropping for their livelihoods.

The iron and steel industries prospered after the Civil War.

Iron and steel manufacturing began to flourish in the northern part of the state. In 1870, two railroads laid tracks in Jones Valley

to serve this growing activity. In 1871, land speculators took a chance on the new industry and founded the town of Birmingham—named for an important industrial city in England. Tannehill Ironworks, located in the small community of Bessemer, had been a major supplier of cannonballs and gun parts during the Civil War. After the war, Bessemer began to produce steel. Bessemer and Birmingham—along with Anniston, Gadsden, and Ensley—became industrial boomtowns. Alabamians needed the work, and the nation needed the iron and steel.

By the 1880s, the entire nation was undergoing what came to be known as the Industrial Revolution. Other industries began to develop in Alabama, including railroading, shipping, lumbering, and textile manufacturing.

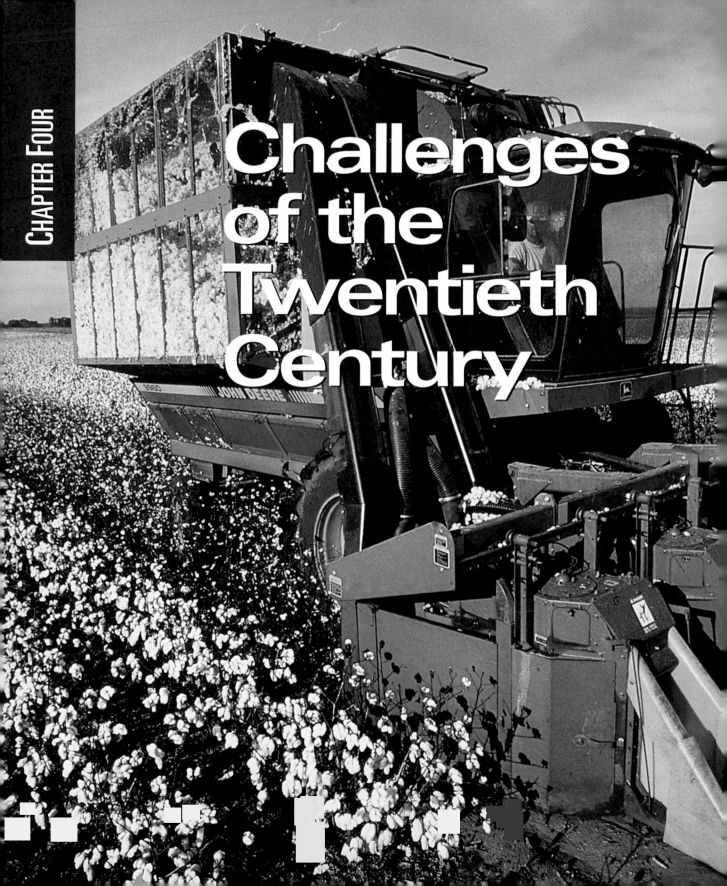

Chapter Four

Challenges of the Twentieth Century

As Alabama entered the twentieth century, it continued to grow. Although more industries developed, the state was still dependent on cotton for its economic stability. Nine-tenths of its population relied on farming for a living—that is, until a destructive little beetle found its way into Alabama's cotton fields.

African-Americans, such as these sharecroppers, had difficult lives.

Throughout most of the twentieth century, life for the state's African-American population continued to be a struggle. A new state constitution made it even harder. Alabama had to pass through a century full of political and social chaos and two world wars before conditions began to change for the better.

A Step Backward

Since 1874, Alabama's state government had been in the hands of wealthy whites who had supported the Confederacy and who still opposed the granting of citizens' rights to African-Americans. These politicians passed laws to keep the races separate in trains, rest rooms, schools, theaters, and other public places. In 1896, the U.S. Supreme Court had approved segregation as long as the facilities were "separate but equal"—although this was rarely the case. Segregation effectively made African-Americans second-class citizens.

Opposite: Harvesting ripe cotton

In 1901, Alabama's new state constitution made life even harder for African-Americans. Until enactment of this new constitution, many African-Americans had exercised their right to vote. The 1901 constitution, however, introduced measures that made it difficult for African-Americans and poor whites to vote. The requirements for voting privileges included the paying of a poll tax, proof of literacy, and, in some cases, proof of solvency (the ability to pay debts) or land ownership. For the next fifty years, only about 5 percent of the state's eligible African-Americans were able to vote in any election.

A boll weevil

The Evil Boll Weevil

The boll weevil is a beetle whose young feed on the boll, or blossom, of the cotton plant. If not exterminated, these hungry little bugs can destroy entire cotton harvests. In 1913, boll weevils came to Alabama from Mexico by way of Texas. In 1915, they swept across the state, destroying the cotton crop and the economy. The plague was actually a blessing in disguise. Because the cotton was ruined, Alabama farmers were forced to plant other crops. Peanuts were introduced as a commercial crop, and today, Alabama ranks second to Georgia in peanut production.

After the weevil blight, cotton again became a valuable crop, attracting northern textile industries to the state. The textile mill

Hard Labor

By the 1890s, iron and steel making had become the most important industry in Alabama. In 1907, United States Steel, the largest steel company in the country, came to Alabama.

For many years, the growing number of steel plants leased prisoners from the state to do the hard and dirty work of mining the ore. The convicts were often not well treated, however, and some people felt that they were taking jobs away from other citizens. Many people in Alabama opposed the practice of using prisoners to work the mines, and the legislature ended the practice in 1928. ■

owners wanted to take advantage of the state's low labor costs. Even though the mills paid low wages, poor Alabamians preferred working in the mills to sharecropping. Many children also worked in mills, receiving as little as 15 cents a day. There was no federal regulation of child labor until 1938.

War, Disasters, and Depression

Nearly 87,000 Alabamians served their country during World War I (1914–1918). Back at home, the war created economic prosperity for the state. Farmers worked to produce food and cotton for the nation. Steel and textile mills worked night and day to supply the materials needed for the war effort. Shipbuilding became an important industry in Mobile.

After the brief economic boom brought on by World War I, Alabama suffered through crippling natural disasters. In 1929, the Alabama-Tombigbee river system flooded

The flood of 1929 devastated life in many rural areas.

Muscle Shoals and Wilson Dam

In 1916, to meet the needs created by World War I, Congress authorized the building of two nitrate-manufacturing plants on the Tennessee River. Nitrate is a chemical used in making explosives. Congress also authorized the construction of a dam to provide hydroelectric power to the two plants. President Woodrow Wilson chose a stretch of shallow, rock-filled waterway known as Muscle Shoals as the site of the dam and the plants. The dam was later named for him.

The two plants were completed just as the war ended in 1918. Wilson Dam was finished in 1924 and began generating electricity in 1925. The dam and the Muscle Shoals plants were turned over to the Tennessee Valley Authority (TVA), which was created by Congress in 1933. The TVA built additional dams near Wilson Dam to make the waterway safe and navigable and to control floods. ■

southern Alabama and caused about $6 million in damage. Hurricanes and a killer tornado that swept through the state in 1932 brought more death and destruction.

Throughout the early 1930s, Alabama and the rest of the nation sank into economic depression. The Great Depression, which began with the stock market crash of October 1929, brought hard times to everyone in the country. Cotton, which had sold in Alabama for about 40 cents a pound during the war, was worth 5 cents or less a decade later. Banks failed. Factories closed. A steep drop in the prices of produce caused people to lose their farms. Many people became homeless; others left the state looking for work. Everyone suffered.

President Franklin Roosevelt's New Deal programs, which began in 1933, were designed to help. The Farm Security Administration provided food, seed, and tools to poor farmers. The Civilian Conservation Corps and Works Progress Administration employed 70,000 Alabamians in projects that built public roads, government facilities, and parks. The Tennessee Valley Authority (TVA) was established to control and preserve the resources of the river-valley region. Great dams were built along the Tennessee River and its branches, providing power plants and locks and channels for navigation. Completed in the late 1930s, the TVA dam projects provided affordable electricity for people living in the valley.

World War II

During World War II (1939–1945), Alabama sent 288,003 citizens into the armed forces. Hundreds of thousands more contributed to the war effort through factory work and volunteer service. World War II also helped pull Alabama and the rest of the country out of the economic struggles of the depression. In the first half of the 1940s, Alabama factories filled a half a billion dollars' worth of orders for wartime goods.

Sharecroppers found that they could earn good money working in defense plants. This shift in the workforce broke the sharecropper system. It also helped move people from farms to the cities. By the end of the war, 300,000 rural Alabamians had moved to Birmingham, Mobile, Huntsville, and other cities to work in factories.

Alabama's mild climate made year-round military training possible, bringing many important bases, airfields, and training camps to the state. One of these bases was Tuskegee Army Air Field, where the Army Air Corps (the name of the U.S. Air Force at the time) trained African-American pilots. About 1,000 of these pilots, known as the Tuskegee Airmen, served during the war.

Cadets at the
Tuskegee Army Air
Field in 1943

The Space Race

The United States and its allies defeated Germany and the Axis powers. After the war ended, many German scientists came to the United States. They had helped develop Germany's advanced military rocket program. Now, they were willing to help the United States build a rocket to explore outer space.

Dr. Wehrner von Braun and his team of German scientists worked first at a military base in Texas, but in 1950 the team was moved to Redstone Arsenal at Huntsville. The Soviet Union launched the world's first satellite, Sputnik, in 1957. Von Braun's team, afraid that the United States was falling behind in the "space race," redoubled its efforts. They were working to develop a U.S. rocket capable of launching a satellite into orbit.

Within months of the Soviet launch, the Jupiter rocket, which was developed at Huntsville, sent the United States' first satellite, *Explorer I,* into space. That same year, Congress organized the National Aeronautics and Space Administration (NASA) to coordinate the nation's space-exploration effort. In 1960, the George C. Marshall Space Flight Center, NASA's first headquarters, was built at Huntsville. The small town, with its research labs, assembly plants, and launch pads, became known as Rocket City, USA. Huntsville grew into a major research center as scientists and engineers from around the nation moved there to be a part of the new space program.

Rockets on display in Huntsville

Civil Rights in the 1960s

As progressive as Alabama was in space research, the state still held a backward view of the rights and roles of African-Americans. Segregation was still a law in the state, and most whites treated blacks as inferior.

During World War II, many Alabamians had protested the segregated training and segregated living within the armed forces. When these African-American soldiers returned from the war, they hoped to enjoy the benefits of the democracy they had fought so hard to preserve. Many white citizens, however, continued to

Rosa Parks

Rosa McCauley Parks was born on February 4, 1913, in Tuskegee, just east of Montgomery. Her father, James McCauley, was a carpenter. Her mother, Leona Edwards McCauley, was a schoolteacher.

In 1932, Rosa married Raymond Parks, a barber and a civil rights activist. They settled in Montgomery. Raymond was active in the National Association for the Advancement of Colored People (NAACP), and Rosa joined the organization, too. She was also very active in the Montgomery Voters League, which helped black citizens pass the many tests required before they could register to vote.

Although Rosa usually walked home from the department store where she worked as a seamstress, on December 1, 1955, she was tired and decided to take the bus. When she was ordered to give up her seat to a white man — which was the law in Alabama — she refused. Her protest and arrest led to the Montgomery bus boycott, marking the beginning of the civil rights movement that swept the country. ■

favor segregation or simply believed it was too hard to change the old system.

The system finally began to crack, however, on December 1, 1955, when Rosa Parks, an African-American woman, refused to give up her seat on the bus to a white man. By law, African-Americans were required to give up their seats to white people traveling by public transportation. Black citizens were also required to sit at the back of the bus. Rosa Park's refusal to move from her seat ignited long-simmering resentments. Parks was arrested, and as her trial worked its way through the legal system, African-Americans refused to ride the buses in Montgomery. A young Baptist minister named Dr. Martin Luther King Jr. led the bus boycott. Some white community members also supported the protest, which lasted for 382 days.

Dexter Avenue King Memorial Baptist Church in Montgomery

When the boycott ended, the Supreme Court ruled that bus segregation was unconstitutional. Rosa Parks and Dr. Martin Luther King Jr. had become nationally recognized civil rights leaders. Alabama, along with its neighbor Mississippi, was now at the center of the nation's civil rights movement.

The Struggles Continue

In 1963, a federal judge ordered the University of Alabama to enroll two black students. Despite a 1954 Supreme Court ruling to integrate public schools, few African-American students were being admitted to southern universities. Governor George C. Wallace, who proclaimed "segregation forever" at his inauguration, personally barred the black students from entering the university. President John F. Kennedy ordered the Alabama National Guard to the site, and Governor Wallace stepped aside and allowed the students to enter.

Dr. Martin Luther King Jr. leading civil rights marchers from Selma to Montgomery

That year, more demonstrations followed. During a peaceful civil rights demonstration in Birmingham, city officials turned fire hoses on the demonstrators. Many of the protesters were badly hurt. A fire bomb at a black church killed four young girls.

In 1964, Congress passed the Civil Rights Act, which banned discrimination on the basis of color, race, national origin, religion, or sex. The act guaranteed equal access to public facilities, the right to vote, and employment opportunities. Any federally funded, national, state, or local program could not discriminate against any group of people. Although this legislation overruled state laws, many states—particularly those in the South—were slow to enforce it.

The Selma Marches

By 1965, Alabama buses had been integrated, the University of Alabama had admitted black students, white establishments had begun serving black customers—but most

African-Americans were still unable to vote. To protest this situation, Martin Luther King Jr. and the Southern Christian Leadership Conference organized a march from Selma to the state capitol in Montgomery, 50 miles (80 km) away.

On March 7, hundreds of citizens marched across the Edmund Pettus Bridge in Selma on their way to Montgomery. On the far side of the bridge, the demonstrators were met by troopers on foot and an all-white volunteer posse on horseback. The marchers were ordered to turn back. When they refused, they were beaten and tear-gassed by the troopers and posse. The attack was seen on nationwide television and reported in newspapers all across the country. That day became known as Bloody Sunday.

Two weeks later, on March 21, King planned another march for voting rights. This time, more than 3,000 people set out, and people came from all over the country to support them. President Lyndon Johnson sent National Guard troops to protect the marchers. The marchers arrived in Montgomery five days later. King addressed a crowd of more than 20,000 people gathered in front of the state capitol.

THE SELMA MOVEMENT
(The Beginning)

The major civil rights protest, which focused national attention on the issue of racial discrimination in voting & led to the passage of the Voting Rights Act of 1965, was centered in Selma.

In January of 1963 local citizens organized a voter registration class & by February others were in Selma to assist with registration. Local law officials & blacks seeking to register to vote soon clashed & this received widespread news coverage.

Dr. Martin Luther King, Jr. came to Selma in January of 1965 to lead the drive for the vote. This began the marches to the Dallas County Courthouse, the great number of arrests, the ensuing violence, & the national media attention on Selma & the issue of voter registration.

ERECTED 1980 BY THE CITY OF SELMA

On a street in Selma, a sign memorializes the historic march that lead to the passage of the Voting Rights Act of 1965.

Martin Luther King Jr.

Martin Luther King Jr., one of the principal leaders of the American civil rights movement, was born in Atlanta, Georgia, on January 15, 1929. He never finished high school because his high scores on college-entrance exams allowed him to enter college at the age of fifteen. King earned a Ph.D. in theology from Boston University. In 1953, he married Coretta Scott of Marion, Alabama. The next year, the Dexter Avenue Baptist Church in Montgomery asked him to become their pastor.

King's work in the Montgomery bus boycott in 1955 and the Selma marches for voting rights in 1965 placed him in the national spotlight as a civil rights leader. In 1957, he helped found the Southern Christian Leadership Conference (SCLC). In 1959, he resigned as church pastor to devote his time to directing the activities of the SCLC.

King traveled throughout the South, advocating nonviolent protest. He was awarded the Nobel Peace Prize in 1964 for his civil rights work. In 1968, he was assassinated in Memphis, Tennessee, where he was leading sanitation workers in a protest over low wages and poor working conditions. ◼

In August, President Johnson signed the Voting Rights Act of 1965. The act banned the poll tax, property qualifications, and other obstacles that kept African-Americans from registering to vote. The march from Selma had been a success.

Shifts in Politics

The Supreme Court rulings and the protests of the 1960s helped African-Americans throughout the nation to claim their right to vote. By the late twentieth century, the percentage of blacks registered to vote in Alabama increased fivefold. In 1964, the Supreme Court made another ruling that was important for voters in Alabama. In the case of *Sims* v. *Reynolds,* the court declared that Alabama's voting districts were drawn to favor some areas over others. The state was ordered to redraw its districts. This made it easier for African-Americans to win state and local elections.

Lucius Amerson was elected sheriff of Macon County in 1966—the first African-American to hold such an office in the South since Reconstruction. The first African-American mayor in Alabama was Johnny Ford, who was elected in 1972 at age twenty-nine. He presided over Tuskegee for six four-year terms. In 1973, he founded the National Conference of Black Mayors, which today has 413 members. In 1979, African-American politician Richard Arrington was elected mayor of Birmingham. African-Americans continue to play an increasingly important role in local and state politics.

Economic Changes

In addition to social and political changes, Alabama also experienced economic changes during the last half of the twentieth century. Alabama, like many other states, faced financial difficulties during the 1980s and early 1990s. In 1980, the state legislature had to increase taxes on cigarettes and alcohol to fund government services, such as state-supported nursing homes and public education.

Since the mid-1970s, heavy manufacturing has decreased in importance, and cotton production no longer drives the state's economy. In fact, products of any kind make up less than 25 percent of the gross state product (GSP). The coal industry has been spurred by the high costs of petroleum and natural gas, however.

In the 1970s, Huntsville experienced the growth of high-technology industries, including computer design and production. During the same period, Birmingham's economy became predominantly service-based. Today, many Alabamians make their living in service industries, which contribute 70 percent of the gross state product. One of Alabama's largest service industries is computer communications. The Alabama Supercomputer Authority (ASA) already has the state government, schools, and businesses wired for progress.

Hopes for the New Century

After the turmoil of the 1960s, tension between the races eased, and the population of Alabama started to grow again. In 1960, the population was estimated at 3,266,740. By 1990, the U.S. census reported that it had grown to 4,062,608. Some of this growth was due to reverse migration. Many African-Americans who had left the state to escape discrimination returned to the state that they had always called home.

Although Alabama's progress has been slow and its history has been troubled, it has made significant strides in the quality of life for its black citizens and in its economic growth and development. There are still many improvements to be made—in education, church desegregation, and reduction of poverty—but the people of the state are working together to shape a better future. Realizing there is still much work to be done, citizens of Alabama are proud to call their capital the Cradle of the Confederacy and the Birthplace of the Civil Rights Movement.

Relaxing in Linn Park, Birmingham

CHAPTER FIVE

Land,
Sea,
and Sky

Little River Canyon

On November 13, 1833, nature provided the people of Alabama with an incredible light show. A meteor shower filled the night sky. Since then, family and regional histories have been reckoned from the night "stars fell" on Alabama.

Throughout its history, nature has provided Alabama with many incredible displays. The state is blessed with a diversity of natural resources. A network of rivers provides the state with abundant fresh water and recreational opportunities. Vast deposits of "red rock," called hematite, provide the ore that has allowed the state to build its iron and steel industries. A wealth of plants, trees, and flowers blanket the state in natural beauty. Wildlife preserves, caves, and caverns fill Alabama with mystery and wonder.

The Lay of the Land

Like a table picked up by one corner, Alabama slants gently from the Appalachian Mountains in the northeast to the Bay of Mobile

Opposite: Overlooking Mount Cheaha State Park

Alabama's gulf coast

Natural Bridge

Natural Bridge of Alabama is the longest natural-rock arch east of the Rocky Mountains. Located in Winston County, it is 148 feet (45 m) long, 33 feet (10 m) wide, 8 feet (3 m) thick, and 60 feet (18 m) high. The sandstone bridge is topped with the fossil of a tree that has been traced back 4 billion years. ■

in the southwest. The state is divided into six land regions: the Cumberland Plateau, the Interior Low Plateau, the Piedmont, the Appalachian Ridge and Valley Region, the Black Belt, and the East Gulf Coastal Plain.

The Cumberland Plateau, also known as the Appalachian Plateau, reaches from the northeast corner to the center of the state. This region contains the southern tip of the Appalachian Mountain range. The Interior Low Plateau, in the northwest part of the state, is the valley of the Tennessee River. Because it is irrigated by the Tennessee waterways, this region is good farming country.

The Piedmont is in the east-central region of Alabama. It is made up of low hills and high ridges separated by sandy valleys. Most of the land is forested. The highest point in the state, Cheaha Mountain at 2,407 feet (734 m), rises on the northwestern edge of the Piedmont. In addition to coal, iron ore, and limestone, this region contains a large deposit of high-quality marble.

In the central part of the state, just northwest of the Piedmont, lies the Appalachian Ridge and Valley. Large deposits of coal, iron ore, and limestone in this region provide all three of the basic elements for making iron and steel.

The Black Belt is a narrow strip of rolling prairie—a black finger of land stretching from the west-central area of the state through the middle of the East Gulf Coastal Plain. The region is named for its sticky, black, clay soils. Many cotton plantations thrived in the rich soils of the Black Belt.

Fields in northwestern Alabama

Topographical map of Alabama

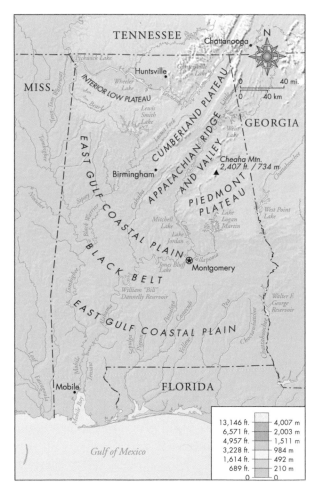

The East Gulf Coastal Plain is the largest region in Alabama. It covers most of the southern two-thirds of the state, except for the area covered by the Black Belt, which cuts across it. The plain extends north almost to Tennessee. This region has several distinct sections: the Mobile River Delta, the Wiregrass area in the southeast, the Central Pine Belt in the north, and the Western Sandy Plains. The lowest elevation in the state is in the Mobile area of this region, which lies at sea level.

Waterways

Alabama has about 1 million acres (405,000 ha) of water. These waters provide weekend fun for tourists and residents, but they also supply power and water to Alabama's businesses and industries. More than 1,600 miles (2,575 km) of Alabama's waters are navigable, and about 1,350 miles (2,172 km) of

Backpacking along Alabama's rivers

river support commercial shipping. California is the only state with more navigable river miles.

Alabama has two major river systems: The Mobile-Tensaw River and the Tennessee River. The Mobile-Tensaw River system flows to the south, draining Alabama's waters to the Gulf of Mobile. The Tennessee River system flows east to west across the northern part of the state. It drains the Cumberland Plateau in a wide, wandering V pattern. The most important electric-power dams in the state are along this river. A number of lakes were created by form-

Treasures of the Cahaba River

The Cahaba River, which starts northeast of Birmingham and runs to Selma, is known as "Alabama's most floated river." It is the state's largest free-flowing stream and a favorite spot for scenic wildlife tours. The river contains 131 different species of fish—more species per mile than any river in the United States.

The Cahaba also contains rare and exotic examples of marine plant life, such as the Cahaba, or Shoals, lilies. These lilies are a threatened species that grow in only a few waterways. The U.S. Fish and Wildlife Service has placed the Cahaba lilies and eleven of the river's fish and freshwater mussel species on lists of endangered or threatened species. Conservationists have formed the Cahaba River Society to preserve the river's natural beauty and resources. ■

ing dams along the Tennessee—the largest is Guntersville Lake, which covers 110 square miles (285 sq km).

The Tombigbee and the Alabama Rivers are the state's major internal rivers. They are also Alabama's longest rivers and come together in one of the most complicated river systems in the country. South past this junction, the Tombigbee is called the Mobile River, and the Alabama is known as the Tensaw River. These two rivers join several times in a crisscrossing of bayous and channels. They flow into Mobile Bay and form two large deltas. A delta is a piece of triangular-shaped land where a river deposits mud, sand, and gravel as it enters a larger body of water.

A smaller, independent river system drains the southeast corner of the state. The Pea and Choctawhatchee Rivers and the Conecuh River and its tributaries—the Sepulga, the Pigeon,

Young bald eagles on a tower above the Alabama River

Alabama's Geographical Features

Total area; rank	52,237 sq. mi. (135,294 sq km); 30th
Land; rank	50,750 sq. mi. (131,444 sq km); 28th
Water; rank	1,487 sq. mi. (3,851 sq km); 20th
Inland water; rank	968 sq. mi. (2,507 sq km); 23rd
Coastal water; rank	519 sq. mi. (1,344 sq km); 12th
Geographic center	Chilton, 12 miles (19 km) southwest of Clanton
Highest point	Cheaha Mountain, 2,407 feet (734 m)
Lowest point	Sea level along the Gulf of Mexico
Largest city	Birmingham
Population; rank	4,062,608 (1990 census); 22nd
Record high temperature	112°F (44°C) at Centreville on September 5, 1925
Record low temperature	–27°F (–33°C) at New Market on January 30, 1966
Average July temperature	80°F (27°C)
Average January temperature	46°F (8°C)
Average annual precipitation	56 inches (142 cm)

and the Patsaliga—run south into Florida's panhandle. Alabama's southern rivers are generally slower and have fewer rocks and rapids than the rivers in the north. These small rivers are popular for fishing and canoeing.

A gray fox

Most of the lakes in Alabama have been formed by damming the large rivers. Demopolis Dam, completed in 1962, created Demopolis Lake along the Black Warrior River. Close to Birmingham are Bankhead Lake on the Black Warrior and Smith Reservoir on the Sipsey River. The Coosa River has five lakes: Lake Jordan, Lake Logan Martin, Mitchell Lake, Lay Lake, and Weiss Lake.

Wild Alabama

Two-thirds of Alabama is covered by forests, which are filled with bears, bobcats, gray and red foxes, and poisonous snakes—such as

An eastern bluebird

rattlers, moccasins, and corals. Of course, there are also deer, squirrel, rabbits, and wild turkeys. The state's conservation program, called Forever Wild, helps preserve and manage the plentiful wildlife.

Bird-watchers love Alabama. In the 1980s, the state made an effort to preserve its wild nesting areas through land-preserve and conservation programs. These efforts have restored the populations of bald eagles, bluebirds, ospreys, great blue herons, and brown pelicans.

Whether from a boat or a pier, thigh-deep in water or lazing on the shore, tourists love to fish in the state's lakes and rivers. There is year-round open season on game fish, such as bass, catfish, crappie, bluegill, and trout. One word of caution: Watch out for the alligators!

The mild climate of Alabama encourages abundant plant life. There are more than 125 different kinds of trees in the state, including pines, oaks, hickories, sweet gum, black walnut, red cedar, cypress, and pecan. Alabama is famous for its azaleas, but it is filled with other green and flowering shrubs, too—such as dog-

Dismals and the Dismalites

Dismals Canyon is located 5 miles (8 km) from Phil Campbell, a town in northwest Alabama. These 80 acres (33 ha) of undisturbed wilderness contain a natural arboretum of twenty-seven varieties of trees that grow within a radius of 100 feet (31 m). Dismals Canyon, which has been declared a national natural landmark, also contains seven natural bridges, waterfalls, cliffs, and a winding natural staircase surrounded by natural rock.

The Dismalites are worms that mysteriously glow in the dark. You can find them in Dismals Canyon, too. ■

wood, mountain laurel, and rhododendron. Throughout the year, but particularly in the spring, the state is bright with the many colors of its wild and cultivated flowers. A large variety of lilies, orchids, and roses fill the formal gardens; wildflowers, such as thistle, pinks, and prairie clover are found in wild plateaus and wooded areas.

Rhododendrons in the woods

DeSoto State Park

DeSoto State Park covers 5,067 acres (2,051 ha) along Little River Canyon—the deepest canyon between the Mississippi River and the Atlantic Ocean. Natural sites in the park area include caves, an onyx cavern, waterfalls, and white-water rivers. The park's unique ecosystem draws interest from professional and amateur naturalists.

The Little River Canyon area is a great place to hike, camp, and explore. The park has chalets, family cabins, motels, campsites, trails, and 40 miles (65 km) of scenic roadways. During the summer, the nature center offers nature hikes, educational trail walks, children's day and overnight camps, and naturalists' seminars. ■

Caves and Caverns

Of all Alabama's natural wonders, the most awe-inspiring are its caves and caverns. Few people have seen some of the caves and caverns that lie under portions of the state. Some of the rarest and most endangered species of wildlife live there. The National Speleological Society has its headquarters in Huntsville. Speleology is the scientific study and exploration of caves. Spelunking is the hobby of exploring caves.

Caves form in deep limestone deposits topped with sandstone. When the sandstone cracks, water seeps into the limestone, forming underground streams. The water works its wonders on the limestone to create "frozen rock" waterfalls and spectacular formations called stalactites (mineral deposits that hang down from the roof of the cave) and stalagmites (mineral deposits that stick up from the floor of the cave).

There are two spectacular caverns in Alabama: Cathedral Cavern in the northeast and Rickwood Caverns just above Birmingham. DeSoto State Park is also a great place to go spelunking. The caves there show clear evidence of use by early humans, as well as by European settlers.

Alabama's parks and forests

CHAPTER SIX

Touring Alabama

W hen it comes to vacation spots, Alabama is one of the best-kept secrets in the United States. The state offers natural wonders and outdoor adventure, national landmarks and diverse historic sites, and cities and towns filled with unique points of interest. With its beaches and mountains, caverns and caves, festivals and museums, Alabama is worth a second—and even a third—visit.

A laboratory at Marshall Space Flight Center in Huntsville

Caves, Caverns, and Outer Space

The Appalachian Mountains, in the northeast part of the state, provide adventurers with caves, canyons, and caverns to explore. Campers can climb up into the mountains and down into the caves in natural park preserves. There is also plenty of hiking, river rafting, and fishing.

Russell Cave National Monument is one of several parks in the northeast tip of the state. Native Americans traveling through the area more than 9,000 years ago camped on this site. The park's visitor's center houses a museum full of objects that these early travelers left behind. Other caverns, caves, and parks in this region are Cathedral Caverns, Sequoyah Caverns, DeSoto State Park, and Little River Canyon National Preserve.

Huntsville, west of Cathedral Caverns, is home to the Marshall Space Flight Center, where the National Aeronautics and Space Administration (NASA) conducts rocket testing. The space

Opposite: Birmingham skyline at sunset

Sequoyah's Contribution

Sequoyah (also spelled Sequoya) was the son of a British trader and a Cherokee woman. Born in 1760 in eastern Tennessee, he moved to Alabama as a young man. Sequoyah, who did not speak, write, or read English, became interested in the "white man's talking leaf" (writing of the English language). The Cherokee did not have a written language. In 1821, Sequoyah created eighty-six symbols to represent all the speech sounds of the Cherokee language.

Because of Sequoyah's syllabary, or alphabet, the Cherokee were able to learn to read and write. Soon, they began publishing books and newspapers in their own language.

The Sequoyah Caverns in Alabama and two parks in California are named for Sequoyah. A county in Oklahoma is also named in his honor. He died in 1843. ■

museum contains a large collection of items, models, and pictures from America's space program—including an *Apollo 16* capsule. Huntsville is also home to the Alabama Supercomputer Center (ASC). The center supports research, education, and Internet access for businesses, state government agencies, public and private schools, and universities.

High-tech Huntsville had a very modest beginning. In 1805, John Hunt from Virginia chose this spot in the valley as a good place to settle. It was an early capital of Alabama Territory. One of the town's historic districts is Alabama Constitution Village, a time capsule of 1819, the year that delegates met there to draft the state's first constitution.

Historical Sites, National Landmarks

A few miles west of Huntsville is historic Mooresville, the oldest town in Alabama. Established in 1818, the town is listed on the National Register of Historic Places.

The city of Florence, in the northwest corner of the state, holds a number of attractions. Among them is the Indian Mound and Museum, a preserved ceremonial mound with artifacts dating from the Paleolithic to Mississippian periods (1,000 B.C. to A.D. 800). Another important site is Pope's Tavern, a hospital built by slaves but tending to the wounded on both sides during the Civil War. Now a history museum, the historic building displays artifacts and furniture from the nineteenth century.

Tuscumbia, a few miles south of Florence, is the birthplace of Helen Keller, the well-known writer and advocate for the sight and hearing impaired. Her childhood home, Ivy Green, is preserved in the style of the late nineteenth century—the era in which she lived there—and is open to the public. *The Miracle Worker,* a stage play about Keller's early life and her influential teacher, is presented at Ivy Green every summer.

Between the towns of Tuscumbia and Cullman is the William B. Bankhead National Forest. The site was named for the Alabama politician who served as Speaker of the U.S. House of Representatives from 1936 to 1940. The Sipsey Wilderness Area within the forest has the last stand (180,684 acres, or 73,177 ha) of old-growth hardwood trees in Alabama.

Helen Keller

Born in 1880, Helen Adams Keller became blind, deaf, and mute at the age of nineteen months, after suffering a high fever during an illness. She learned to read, write, and speak through the efforts of her teacher, Anne Sullivan.

Keller graduated cum laude from Radcliffe College in Mass-achusetts. She spent her life working to improve conditions for the sight and hearing impaired. She helped found and served as a member of the Massachusetts Commission for the Blind. Through her lectures and stage appearances, she raised money for the American Foundation for the Blind.

Her travels took her around the world, where she received awards and honors from foreign governments and international organizations. She wrote six books including her autobiography, *The Story of My Life,* published in 1903, and *Helen Keller's Journals,* published in 1938. She died in 1968. ■

The town of Cullman was founded as a German colony in 1873 by Colonel John Cullmann. Cullman County Museum and Ave Maria Grotto—which is on the National Registry of Historic Sites—are among its major attractions.

Cullman marks the start of "covered bridge country." Outside of Cullman are a number of historic covered bridges, including the Clarkson and the Blount County Covered Bridges. In October, the area hosts an annual Covered Bridge Festival.

Museums and Magic

Tuscaloosa, Birmingham, and Anniston are three of the major cities located in the central part of the state. Tuscaloosa, now a college town, was the capital of Alabama from 1826 to 1846. It is home to the University of Alabama's football team, the Crimson Tide. Its historic sites include the Alabama Museum of Natural History, the Battle–Friedman House, and Old Tavern on Capitol Square.

South of Tuscaloosa is Moundville. Moundville Archaeological Park contains more than twenty flat-topped, earthen mounds. The mounds are spread across 317 acres (128 ha), which also include a museum and a recreated temple. The Moundville Native American Festival takes place in the park in late September every year.

Birmingham, which has been a major steel-producing center for more than a century, was named for England's important industrial city. Nicknamed Magic City because of its tremendous growth soon after its founding in 1871, Birmingham is now Alabama's largest city. The best view of the city is from Red Mountain, where a 55-foot (17-m) iron statue of Vulcan, set on a 124-foot (38-m)

Clark Hall on the University of Alabama campus in Tuscaloosa

pedestal, watches over the city. This statue of the Roman god of fire and metallurgy was made from native Alabama iron for the 1904 Louisiana Purchase Exhibition (World's Fair) in St. Louis, Missouri.

Two museums document the history of the steel-making industry in Birmingham: the Red Mountain Museum and the Sloss Furnaces National Historic Landmark. The city also boasts several other history museums and the Arlington Antebellum Home and Gardens. The Birmingham Civil Rights Institute is the focal point of the Civil Rights District, which includes the historic Sixteenth Street Baptist Church and Kelly Ingram Park.

Anniston, located in the foothills of the Appalachian Mountain range, was the birthplace of the Alabama Shakespeare Festival before the event moved to Montgomery. The Anniston Museum of Natural History displays a re-creation of African wildlife in native settings.

Southwest of Anniston is the town of Talladega, which has two important parks. Talladega National Forest winds through the southern tip of the Appalachian Mountains. DeSoto Caverns Park is the site of a 2,000-year-old Native American burial ground. A onehour tour highlights the cave's place in history and features a laser-light and sound show.

Cradles of Achievement

The city of Montgomery, in the southeastern part of the state, was named for General Richard Montgomery, a hero of the Revolutionary War. Founded in 1819, Montgomery became the capital of the state in 1846. Known as both the Cradle of the Confederacy and

A statue of Vulcan, the Roman god of fire, keeps watch over the city of Birmingham.

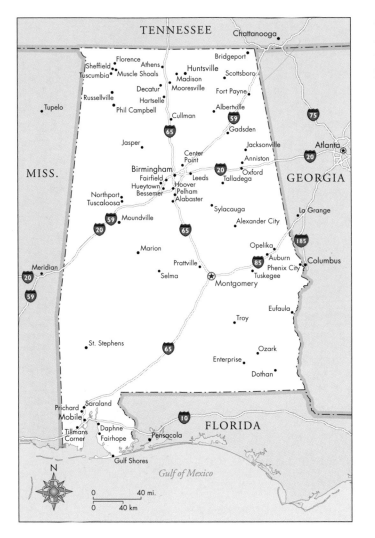

Alabama's cities
and interstates

the birthplace of the Civil Rights Movement, the city has historic sites marking both events.

Montgomery was selected as the first capital of the Confederacy, and Jefferson Davis was inaugurated there. A bronze star marks the spot. The first White House of the Confederacy, President Davis's home, is now a Confederate museum. The state capitol was built in 1851.

The Dexter Avenue King Memorial Baptist Church honors its former pastor, Dr. Martin Luther King Jr., and his leadership in the civil rights struggle. There is a mural depicting events of King's life in the basement of this restored, Victorian-era building. Near the church is the Civil Rights Memorial, designed by Maya Lin, who also designed the Vietnam Veterans Memorial in Washington, D.C.

East of Montgomery is the town of Tuskegee. The town's name comes from the American-Indian word for a village that once stood nearby. It is the home of Tuskegee Institute, founded by educator Booker T. Washington. The institute's campus, the Oaks (which was Washington's residence), and the George Washington Carver Museum are open to the public for tours.

Great Men of Tuskegee Institute

Booker Taliaferro Washington was born in a Virginia slave hut in 1856. His early life of poverty did not allow for regular schooling. Determined to get an education, however, he worked his way through Hampton Normal and Agricultural Institute in Virginia and graduated in 1875. A normal school is a two-year, teacher-training school.

Washington believed the best opportunity for African-Americans was through indus-trial education and land owner-ship. In 1881, he was selected to establish a normal school for African-Americans in Alabama. Tuskegee Normal and Industrial Institute (above left) became his life's work. He died in 1915.

George Washington Carver (in mural, above right) was born a slave in Missouri in 1860. He went to college in Iowa, where he earned a master's degree in science at Iowa State Agricultural College. In 1896, he was appointed head of the department of agriculture at Tuskegee Institute. He spent his life there, teaching and conducting agricultural experiments. In the course of his work, he discovered more than 300 new uses for peanuts and more than 100 new uses for sweet potatoes. His experiments with peanuts, pecans, sweet potatoes, and cotton also led to improvements in farming. He died in Tuskegee in 1943. ■

Dothan, in far-southeast Alabama, is known as the Peanut Capital of the World. The area produces one-fourth of the nation's peanuts. Naturally, the town is the site of the National Peanut Festival. The U.S. Army Aviation museum is in nearby Fort Rucker.

Tracing Historical Footsteps

To travel from Montgomery to Selma requires a trip across the Edmund Pettus Bridge. This route follows the historic path taken by Dr. Martin Luther King Jr. and thousands of other people who marched in support of voting rights in 1965. The National Voting Rights Museum and Institute is also located in Selma.

Mobile is unlike the rest of Alabama. History has given its culture distinctive French and Spanish influences. No discussion of Mobile would be complete without mentioning the festival of Mardi Gras. The French founders started celebrating this holiday in 1703, more than 100 years before the citizens of New Orleans began hosting their own Mardi Gras.

Mobile's history is preserved throughout the city. Fort Conde on South Royal and Church Streets has been reconstructed to look much as it did when it served as the capital of Louisiana Territory.

The USS *Alabama* Battleship Memorial Park proudly displays the World War II battleship. The *Alabama* and the USS *Drum,* a submarine, are open daily for public inspection.

Historic homes in the area include Oakleigh, a beautiful antebellum (pre–American Civil War) mansion, and Carlen House Museum, a simple Creole cottage built in

The Edmund Pettus Bridge as it looks today

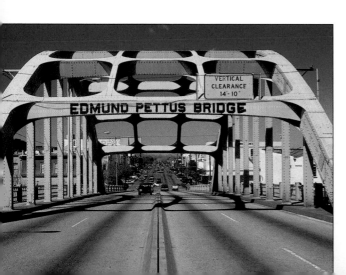

Mardi Gras in Mobile

The name Mardi Gras is French for "Fat Tuesday" (mardi means "Tuesday"; gras means "fat"). Fat Tuesday is the day before Ash Wednesday, which marks the beginning of Lent and Easter, a religious season that observes the death and resurrection of Jesus Christ. The day was called "fat" because it was the last day to celebrate before the required period of fasting began.

When French settlers arrived in Mobile in the eighteenth century, they brought the European tradition of Mardi Gras with them. The festival was suspended during the Civil War, but after the war, a man named Joseph Stillwell Cain revived it as a way to boost morale in Mobile. In honor of Cain, the Sunday before Fat Tuesday is called Joe Cain Day, a time for "raisin' Cain" (acting wildly). ■

1842. Bellingrath Gardens, known for its beautiful displays of azaleas, is south of the city. Fort Gaines and Fort Morgan are also within a short driving distance.

Each October, the town of Gulf Shores, located on the Gulf Coast, hosts the National Shrimp Festival. Gulf State Park, 30 miles (48 km) from Mobile, is a beach resort.

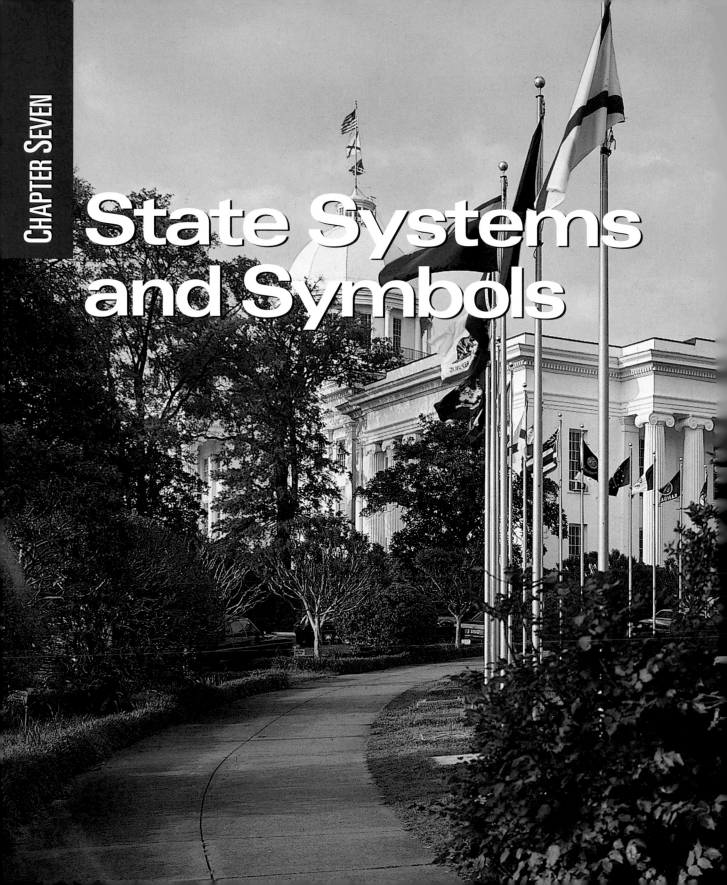

CHAPTER SEVEN

State Systems and Symbols

state government is charged with the business of running the state. A state's constitution contains the guidelines for how the government is to conduct that business. Alabama has had six constitutions. The last one was adopted in 1901. Alabama's constitution is a lengthy document—more than 175,000 words. In fact, it may be one of the longest constitutions in the world. The people of the state of Alabama are working together to improve their government and to change their long—and, some say, not very efficient—state constitution.

The state capitol in Montgomery

The Alabama Constitution Project

One of the reasons that the people of Alabama want a new state constitution is to allow "home rule," or self-governing. Because the cities and counties do not have home rule, any changes in the way they conduct their business requires an amendment to the state's constitution—which is one reason why the constitution has become so long.

Alabamians are serious about rewriting their constitution. In the early 1990s, people and newspapers around the state began the Alabama Constitution Project, a series of electronic town-hall meetings. These meetings are discussions of the many problems created for local and county governments by the lengthy state constitution. Newspaper journalists and political and business leaders have also spoken out for the need to modernize the state's governing document. ■

Opposite: The grounds surrounding the state capitol

Executive Branch

Similar to the government of most other states, Alabama's state government is divided into three branches: executive, legislative, and judicial. The governor, the head of the executive branch, is elected to a four-year term. He or she may serve more than one term. After two consecutive terms, however, the governor must wait four years before serving again. The governor's primary duty is to ensure that the laws of the state are enforced. The governor may approve or veto laws passed by the legislature, call emergency

Four-Term Governor George C. Wallace

George Corley Wallace was born in Clio in 1919. He graduated from the University of Alabama Law School in 1942. He served in the U.S. Army Air Force, in the Alabama state legislature, and as a judge before running for governor in 1958. His first attempt to become elected failed, but he ran again in 1962 and won.

During his first term in office, the state erupted in marches and demonstrations over civil rights issues. Wallace's dramatic "stand in the schoolhouse door" brought him national notoriety as a symbol of the southern white opposition to school integration.

Because the state constitution in 1967 would not allow Wallace to serve another term, he convinced his wife, Lurleen B. Wallace, to run for governor. She won the election, but died before her term was completed. Wallace was elected again in 1971. The constitution had been changed, and Wallace was now able to serve two consecutive terms.

Wallace attempted to run for president of the United States several times. During his 1972 presidential campaign, he was shot by a would-be assassin, Arthur Bremer. Wallace continued his political career from his wheelchair.

Wallace's fourth and last term as governor began in 1983. This term was marked by the complete reversal of his previous political position, and he won a large portion of the African-American vote. Wallace died in 1998. ■

Alabama's Governors

Name	Party	Term	Name	Party	Term
William Wyatt Bibb	Dem.-Rep.	1819–1820	William Calvin Oates	Dem.	1894–1896
Thomas Bibb	Dem.-Rep.	1820–1821	Joseph Forney Johnston	Dem.	1896–1900
Israel Pickens	Dem.-Rep.	1821–1825	William James Samford	Dem.	1900–1901
John Murphy	Dem.-Rep.	1825–1829	William Dorsey Jelks	Dem.	1901–1907
Gabriel Moore	Dem.	1829–1831	Braxton Bragg Comer	Dem.	1907–1911
Samuel B. Moore	Dem.	1831	Emmett O'Neal	Dem.	1911–1915
John Gayle	Dem.	1831–1835	Charles Henderson	Dem.	1915–1919
Clement Comer Clay	Dem.	1835–1837	Thomas Erby Kilby	Dem.	1919–1923
Hugh McVay	Dem.	1837	William W. Brandon	Dem.	1923–1927
Arthur P. Bagby	Dem.	1837–1841	Bibb Graves	Dem.	1927–1931
Benjamin Fitzpatrick	Dem.	1841–1845	Benjamin Meek Miller	Dem.	1931–1935
Joshua Lanier Martin	Dem.	1845–1847	Bibb Graves	Dem.	1935–1939
Reuben Chapman	Dem.	1847–1849	Frank M. Dixon	Dem.	1939–1943
Henry Watkins Collier	Dem.	1849–1853	Chauncey Sparks	Dem.	1943–1947
John Anthony Winston	Dem.	1853–1857	James E. Folsom	Dem.	1947–1951
Andrew Barry Moore	Dem.	1857–1861	Gordon Persons	Dem.	1951–1955
John Gill Shorter	Dem.	1861–1863	James E. Folsom	Dem.	1955–1959
Thomas Hill Watts	Dem.	1863–1865	John M. Patterson	Dem.	1959–1963
Lewis E. Parsons	Dem.	1865	George C. Wallace	Dem.	1963–1967
Robert Miller Patton	Rep.	1865–1867	Lurleen Wallace	Dem.	1967–1968
Military rule		1867–1868	Albert P. Brewer	Dem.	1968–1971
William Hugh Smith	Rep.	1868–1870	George C. Wallace	Dem.	1971–1979
Robert Burns Lindsay	Dem.	1870–1872	Forrest H. James Jr.	Dem.	1979–1983
David Peter Lewis	Rep.	1872–1874	George C. Wallace	Dem.	1983–1987
George Smith Houston	Dem.	1874–1878	Guy Hunt	Rep.	1987–1993
Rufus W. Cobb	Dem.	1878–1882	Jim Folsom	Dem.	1993–1995
Edward Asbury O'Neal	Dem.	1882–1886	Fob James Jr.	Rep.	1995–1999
Thomas Seay	Dem.	1886–1890	Donald Siegelman	Dem.	1999–
Thomas Goode Jones	Dem.	1890–1894			

sessions of the legislature, and grant pardons. The governor also serves as commander in chief of the state militia.

Other state officers in the executive branch are the lieutenant governor, secretary of state, treasurer, attorney general, auditor, and

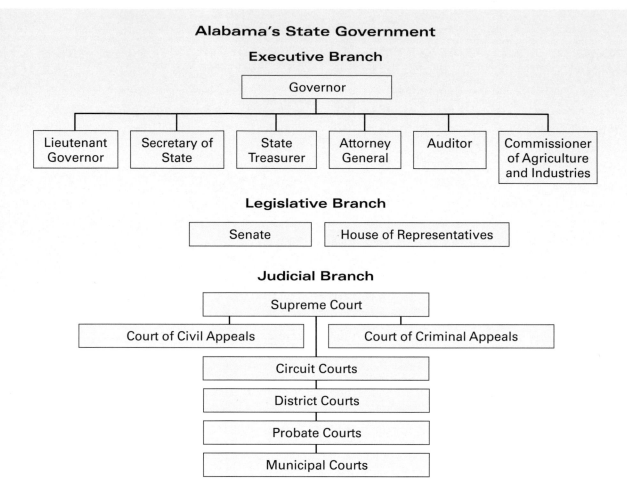

Alabama's State Government

Executive Branch

Governor

Lieutenant Governor | Secretary of State | State Treasurer | Attorney General | Auditor | Commissioner of Agriculture and Industries

Legislative Branch

Senate | House of Representatives

Judicial Branch

Supreme Court

Court of Civil Appeals | Court of Criminal Appeals

Circuit Courts

District Courts

Probate Courts

Municipal Courts

commissioner of agriculture and industries. These officials are also elected to four-year terms.

Legislative Branch

The legislative branch of the state government is responsible for creating the governing laws. The Alabama legislature has two houses: the senate and the house of representatives. There are 35 senators and 105 representatives.

Legislators are elected for four-year terms. The terms are not staggered, which means that all legislators stand for reelection at the same time every four years.

The state constitution may be amended either by the state legislature or by a constitutional convention. An amendment proposed by the legislature must be approved by three-fifths of the members of both the house and the senate. It must then be approved by a majority of the voters in the

A replica of the Liberty Bell in front of Alabama's capitol

Hugo Lafayette Black

Hugo Black was born in Harlan in 1886. He served as a U.S. senator from 1927 to 1937. He was then appointed associate justice of the U.S. Supreme Court, where he served until his death in 1971.

Black served one of the longest terms in the history of the Court. His term was marked by his work in support of the government protection of civil rights. ■

The Scottsboro Case

During the Great Depression of the 1930s, the homeless and unemployed often drifted from town to town looking for work. Sometimes, they traveled by stealing rides in the empty boxcars of railroad trains.

On March 25, 1931, a fight erupted between white and black men who were traveling in the same boxcar. The fight ended when the black men, who were greater in number, threw the white men off the train. Two white women and nine black men were left in the boxcar. When the train stopped, the black men were arrested.

Although medical evidence did not support them, the white women claimed that the black men had assaulted them. The trials before all-white juries lasted three days. The nine black men—one only twelve years old, another almost blind, another disabled—were convicted and sentenced to death.

Through the efforts of the International Labor Defense, the case was taken to the U.S. Supreme Court. In October 1932, the Court reversed the guilty verdict of the men, who had come to be known as the Scottsboro Boys. (Although all of the men were young, the term *boy* was also intended as a racial slur.) The Court ruled that the defendants were not adequately represented by legal counsel in their murder trials—one volunteer lawyer handled all nine cases. The men were retried in 1933.

Although one of the women now denied the assaults, an all-white jury again convicted the black men, asking for the death penalty. The judge refused the verdict, resulting in a third trial that ended with the same result. In April 1935, the Supreme Court again reversed the convictions on the grounds that there were no African-Americans on the juries, which denied the accused a fair trial.

The cycle of trial, conviction, and appeal continued until 1937, when a compromise freed the four youngest defendants. The last man was not released from prison until nineteen years later. The two historic Supreme Court rulings in these cases helped advance the civil rights movement. ■

state. To call a constitutional convention, a majority of the house, senate, and voters must approve.

Judicial Branch

The state judicial branch has a supreme court, a court of civil appeals, and a court of criminal appeals. A chief justice and eight associates preside over the state supreme court. Three judges preside in the court of civil appeals. Five judges rule in the court of criminal appeals. Lower courts include circuit, district, probate, and municipal. All judges and justices are elected to six-year terms.

Local Government

There are sixty-seven counties in Alabama. Each county is governed by a board of commissioners. In most counties, the chief official is the probate judge. Other county officials include the sheriff, district attorney, superintendents of education, engineer, tax assessor, and tax collector.

Alabama's cities are run by various systems of government. A number of cities have a commission form of government, similar to that of the counties. Other cities are run by city

Alabama's counties

Birmingham's city hall

managers. Birmingham, Huntsville, Montgomery, and Tuscaloosa are run by mayors and city councils. Most of the smaller cities and towns are also governed by a mayor and a city council.

Representation

Residents of Alabama who are U.S. citizens may register to vote if they are eighteen years old, have not been convicted of a felony, and have not been judged "mentally incompetent" in a court of law. Prospective voters must be registered to vote ten days before an election. If a registered voter moves to another county, that voter must register again in that county.

Alabama has two U.S. senators and seven representatives. In presidential elections, the state casts nine electoral votes.

State Capitals

Since 1817, when Alabama was first designated a territory, five capitals have served as its seats of government. When the U.S. Congress created the territory, Saint Stephens was designated as the capital. Two sessions of the territorial legislature met there.

The first state constitutional convention met in Huntsville in 1819, and the first session of the general assembly met there that same year. The territorial legislature, however, had chosen Cahaba as the site for the capital. The second general assembly met in Cahaba in 1820. At that session, Cahaba was designated the temporary seat of government in the constitution, giving the 1825–1826 legislature the power to chose a permanent site. It chose Tuscaloosa.

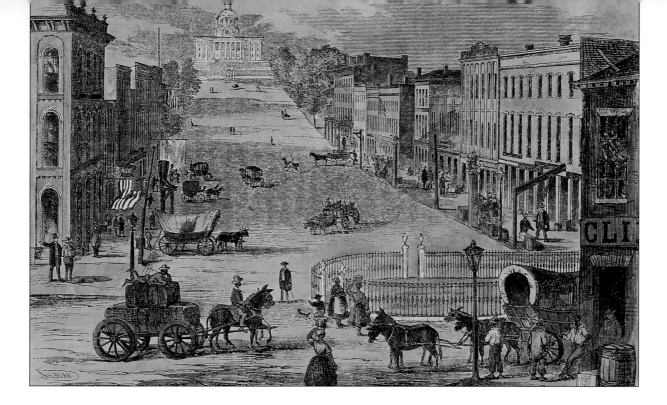

A view of the capitol in Montgomery in 1857

Tuscaloosa remained the capital from 1826 to 1846, when population gains in the eastern part of the state made the site inconvenient. The legislature amended the constitution to allow a change. A number of towns wanted to be the state capital, but after sixteen ballots, Montgomery won.

When selecting Montgomery as the new capital, the legislature ruled that the state should not have to pay to build a capitol. The citizens of Montgomery raised $75,000 in bonds to buy land and construct a capitol. A year later, on December 6, 1847, the city presented the building to the state. Two years later, the new capitol burned. Forced into temporary quarters, the legislature gave in and appropriated $60,000 to construct a new building. What is now the center section of the state capitol was built on the foundation of the burned original. An east wing was added in 1885, a south wing in 1905–1906, and a north wing in 1911. The building was restored and refurbished in 1992.

Alabama's State Symbols

State bird: Yellowhammer Adopted as the state bird in 1927, the yellowhammer is a member of the woodpecker family. It got its name from the yellow coloring under its wings and the way it "hammers" trees with its beak. The bird's colors resembled the uniform of Confederate cavalrymen, and an Alabama regiment of the Confederate Army wore yellowhammer feathers in their hats.

State tree: Southern longleaf pine Twelve species of pine grow in the South, and four are prevalent in Alabama: longleaf, slash, loblolly, and shortleaf. Southern longleaf pine was adopted as the state tree in 1949.

State saltwater fish: Fighting tarpon This saltwater game fish, adopted as the state fish in 1955 and as the state saltwater fish in 1975, can weigh as much as 100 pounds (45 kg).

State freshwater fish: Largemouth bass Abundant in the inland waters and popular with fishing enthusiasts, the largemouth bass became the state freshwater fish in 1975.

State flower: Camellia This flower was adopted by the legislature in 1959. Its colors include white, pink, red, and mixtures. Red and red-and-white camellias recall the bold red and white of the state flag.

State mineral: Hematite This red iron ore has been important to the state's iron and steel industry since 1863. It was designated the state mineral in 1967.

State rock: Marble Many consider Alabama's marble (calcium carbonite) to be of finer quality than Italian marble. The legislature adopted marble as the state rock in 1969.

State nut: Pecan The pecan tree (above) and its thinshelled nut, adopted by the legislature in 1982, is native to America and cultivated throughout Alabama.

State insect: Monarch butterfly The legislature made this native butterfly, which is well known throughout Alabama, the state insect in 1989.

State reptile: Red-bellied turtle Found in the waters of the Mobile Delta, the red-bellied turtle is native to Alabama and has been the state reptile since 1990. It grows up to 13 inches (33 cm) long, and its head, neck, and legs have yellowish stripes.

State gemstone: Star blue quartz The state legislature adopted this stone in 1990.

State shell: Johnstone's Junonia This offshore seashell, common to the Gulf Coast, became the state shell in 1990. A Harvard scientist named it in honor of Kathleen Yerger Johnstone of Mobile, who popularized seashells through her speeches and books.

State nicknames: Heart of Dixie, Cotton State, Yellowhammer State

State motto: We Dare Defend Our Rights The Latin version of the state motto, "Audemus Jura Nostra Defendere," appears on the official coat of arms adopted in 1939. The coat of arms displays the flags of the five nations that have held sovereignty over Alabama: Spain, France, Great Britain, the Confederacy, and the United States. The shield of the United States at the center is supported by two American bald eagles on either side.

Alabama's State Song
"Alabama"

Julia Strudwick Tutwiler, a distinguished educator and humanitarian, wrote the words for the state song. The inspiration for her poem, "Alabama," came to her after she returned from a trip to Germany. Remembering the patriotism of the Germans, kept alive by rousing songs, she thought a state song would help raise the spirits of Alabamians suffering through the Great Depression.

Edna Goeckel Gussen of Birmingham wrote the music for Tutwiler's poem. On March 3, 1931, the words and the music were designated the official state song.

Alabama, Alabama
We will aye be true to thee,
From thy Southern shores where
  groweth,
By the sea thine orange tree.
To thy Northern vale where
  floweth,
Deep and blue thy Tennessee,
Alabama, Alabama
We will aye be true to thee!

Broad the Stream whose name
  thou bearest;
Grand thy Bigbee rolls along;
Fair thy Coosa—Tallapoosa
Bold thy Warrior, dark and strong,
Goodlier than the land that Moses
Climbed lone Nebo's Mount to
  see,
Alabama, Alabama,
We will aye be true to thee!

From thy prairies broad and fer-
  tile,
Where thy snow-white cotton
  shines,

To the hills where coal and iron
Hide in thy exhaustless mines,
Strong-armed miners—sturdy
  farmers;
Loyal hearts what'er we be,
Alabama, Alabama,
We will aye be true to thee!

From thy quarries where the
  marble
White as that of Paros gleams
Waiting till thy sculptor's chisel,
Wake to life thy poet's dreams;
For not only wealth of nature,
Wealth of mind hast thou to
  see,
Alabama, Alabama,
We will aye be true to thee!

Where the perfumed south wind
  whispers,
Thy magnolia groves among,
Softer than a mother's kisses,
Sweeter than a mother's song;
Where the golden jasmine trailing
Woos the treasure-laden bee,

Alabama, Alabama,
We will aye be true to thee!

Brave and pure thy men and women
Better this than corn and wine,
Make us worthy, God in Heaven,
Of this goodly land of Thine,
Hearts as open as our door-ways,
Liberal hands and spirits free,

Alabama, Alabama,
We will aye be true to thee!

Little, little, can I give thee,
Alabama, mother mine;
But that little—hand, brain, spirit,
As I have and am are thine,
Take, O take the gift and giver,
Take and serve thyself with me,
Alabama, Alabama,
I will aye be true to thee!

State Flags and Seal

Alabama did not have a state flag until January 11, 1861, when the legislature designated a flag designed by a group of women from Montgomery. This first flag is known as the Republic of Alabama Flag.

One side of the flag displayed the Goddess of Liberty holding an unsheathed sword in her right hand and a small flag with one star in her left. The phrase "Independent Now and Forever" arched over her head. On the other side of the flag was a cotton plant with a coiled rattlesnake. Beneath the cotton plant were the Latin words *Noli Me Tangere* (Touch Me Not). This flag flew until February 10, 1891, when it was retired after being damaged in a storm. It never flew again.

Alabama's new state flag was authorized by the state legislature on February 16, 1895. The flag displays the crimson cross of St. Andrew on a field of white and is patterned after the Confederate battle flag.

Alabama's state seal contains two concentric circles with the words "Alabama Great Seal" between them. Inside the circles is a map showing Alabama's principal rivers, the four bordering states (Mississippi, Tennessee, Georgia, and Florida), and the Gulf of Mexico. The seal was designed by William W. Bibb, the state's first governor. Alabama's state seal is the only one in the country to contain a map of the state as part of its design. ■

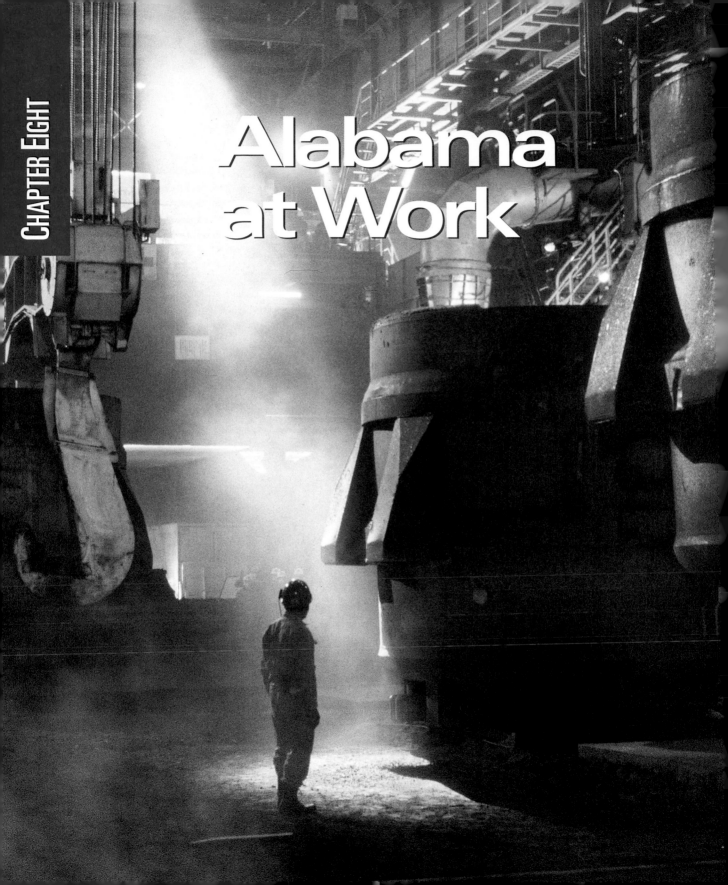

CHAPTER EIGHT

Alabama at Work

A peach orchard

Throughout the nineteenth century, King Cotton ruled as Alabama's cash crop and economic support. Farming kept Alabamians employed and fed. The state no longer depends on farming as its main source of income, however. Today, the service industries, including those in government and trade, account for 70 percent of the gross state product—the values of goods and services produced in the state in a year. Cotton is still one of Alabama's many important farm products, however. Alabama is the ninth-largest producer of cotton in the nation.

Farms and Forests

After the invasion of the boll weevil destroyed Alabama's cotton fields in 1915, the state's farmers began planting other crops and raising livestock (cattle, hogs, and poultry). There are poultry farms in the north, and beef cattle are raised in the north and central Black Belt counties. Hog-producing farms are found in the southeastern

Opposite: Iron- and steel-making industries are located in the northern part of the state.

counties. Today, livestock sales account for more than two-thirds of the total farm-products sales in the state. Broilers (chicken) account for 40 percent of the farm income. Alabama is second in the country in the production of broilers.

Alabama farms produce varied agricultural goods. The greatest amount of acreage is devoted to growing soybeans and corn, which are planted in the southern part of the state. Alabama is the second-largest producer of peanuts and the sixth-largest producer of pecans in the country. Peanuts are grown in the southeastern counties; pecans are produced throughout most parts of the state. Other important farm crops include hay, oats, sorghum, tobacco, and wheat.

Fruits and vegetables are also produced in Alabama. Greenhouses in Cullman and Limestone Counties in the northern part of the state produce strawberries. Peaches and apples are grown in Blount County in the north and Chilton County in the central part

Sorghum

Sorghum is a grass plant that is similar to Indian corn. It is grown as a grain product and is often used as cattle feed. A variety of this plant, called sorgo, is grown for the sweet juices in the stem. Sugar and a dark syrup are made from sorgo.

of the state. Other fruit and vegetable crops include watermelons, pears, beans, cucumbers, potatoes, sweet potatoes, and tomatoes.

Most of Alabama's farms are large-scale, mechanized operations. Farmland covers about 30 percent of the state. Nearly 47,000 farms work 11 million acres (4.5 million ha). The average farm size is 213 acres (86 ha). Although farming is big business in Alabama, it only accounts for 2 percent of the gross state product.

In the 1980s, Alabama began a conservation program of forest management and replanting. As a result, the state has increased its commercial forest area. Today, Alabama has 22 million acres (9 million ha) of forestland for logging. The state provides pine and hardwood to commercial lumber operations. Pulpwoods are provided to make paper products, the leading category of manufactured goods in the state.

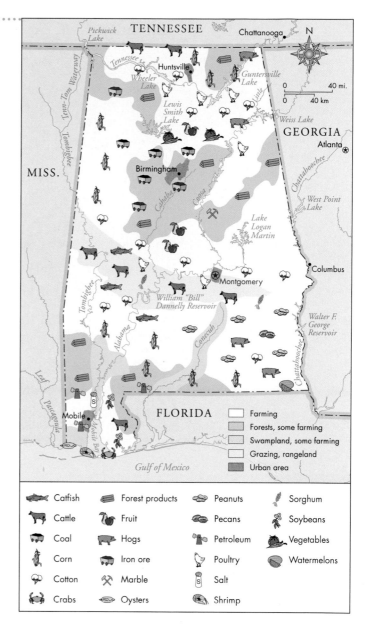

Alabama's natural resources

Service Industries

Service industries provide the main support for Alabama's economy. Businesses and organizations in the service industry include

What Alabama Grows, Manufactures, and Mines

Agriculture	Manufacturing	Mining
Chicken	Paper products	Coal
Beef cattle	Chemicals	Natural gas
Greenhouse and nursery products	Textiles	Petroleum
	Primary metals	Crushed stone
Eggs	Food products	Limestone
Peanuts	Clothing	Marble

wholesale and retail trade; community, social, and personal services; government services; and finance, insurance, and real estate. Most service industries are located in large cities or metropolitan areas.

The leading industry is wholesale and retail trade, followed closely by community, business, personal, and government services. Alabama's wholesale trade is centered in Mobile. Government services include public schools, public hospitals, and military operations. The leading employer in the state is the public-school system. Major military bases include Fort McClellan in Anniston in the eastern part of the state, and Fort Rucker near Dothan in the southeast corner. Gunter and Maxwell Air Force Bases are near Montgomery. In the north, close to Huntsville, is the George C. Marshall Space Flight Center. The Redstone Arsenal is also located there.

Medical facilities, law firms, and engineering companies are some of the community, social, and personal services operating in Alabama. Blount, one of the largest con-

Troops at Fort McClellan

struction engineering companies in the nation, is based in Montgomery. Montgomery is also the headquarters for Alfa Insurance, a national company. Many of the state's financial institutions are located in Birmingham. Amsouth and SouthTrust, two of the South's largest banks, are headquartered there.

Ranked fifth among the service industries are transportation, utilities, and communication. Mobile is one of the main shipping ports in the United States. It is also

Ships docked in Mobile Bay

Winton "Red" Blount

In 1946, Winton Blount and his brother, Houston, founded Blount Brothers Corporation, a small construction company in Union Springs. Today, the company—Blount International, headquartered in Montgomery—is one of the largest construction companies in the nation. It manufactures and distributes products in more than 100 countries throughout the world and employs more than 6,000 people. The company helped construct portions of the John F. Kennedy Space Center in Florida.

Always an active civic and business leader in Alabama, Winton Blount was elected president of the U.S. Chamber of Commerce in 1968. President Richard Nixon then appointed him postmaster general, a position he held from 1969 to 1971. After leaving Washington, Blount returned to Alabama to run his company and continue his civic work.

The Alabama Shakespeare Festival is held in the $22-million performing-arts complex in Montgomery that Blount and his wife, Carolyn, donated. Their gift was the largest single donation ever made to an American theater company. ■

Tennessee-Tombigbee Waterway

The Tennessee-Tombigbee Waterway is a shipping lane for products moving from the mid-south region of the country to the Gulf of Mexico. During the 1988 drought along the Mississippi River, the Ten-Tom, as it is popularly known, carried the commercial shipping that the Mississippi could not.

The Ten-Tom took almost three centuries to create. The idea for a water route linking the country's fourteen major river systems was presented in the early eighteenth century. In 1810, the U.S. Congress considered it again, but did not go ahead with the project until 1946. The Ten-Tom opened in 1985.

Because of its design, the Ten-Tom is almost drought-free. A 39-mile (63-km) Divide Cut joins the Tennessee and Tombigbee Rivers to create the waterway. More than 150 cubic yards (115 cu m) of earth were removed to make the Cut—twice the amount of earth removed to create the Panama Canal.

The Ten-Tom can move 32 million tons of cargo annually. There are seventeen new commercial ports along the waterway. Industrial sites along the Ten-Tom are flood-free and have direct railroad service. Although a large portion of the Ten-Tom is in Tennessee and Mississippi, the last leg of the journey to the Gulf of Mexico is through Alabama. ■

one of the busiest. There are about 1,350 miles (2,172 km) of navigable waterways in Alabama. These waterways provide transportation for products moving through the southern states. Alabama also depends on truck and train transportation. Most of the state's air traffic is concentrated at the large airports in Birmingham, Huntsville, and Mobile.

Two major phone companies, South Central Bell and Bell-South, are headquartered in Birmingham. Electrical-power utilities in the state produce electricity by burning coal, through nuclear reaction, or with water power (hydroelectricity). Coal-burning plants produce 70 percent of the state's electricity.

Communications organizations include newspapers and radio and television stations throughout the state. *The Mobile Register,* founded in 1813, is Alabama's oldest newspaper. There are more than 100 newspapers published in Alabama. Thirty of them are published daily. *The Birmingham News* has the largest circulation.

Alabama has about 230 radio stations. Begun as WMAV in Auburn in 1922, WAPI in Birmingham is the state's oldest commercial radio station. Alabama's first television station, WVTM-TV, located in Birmingham, went on the air in May 1949 as WABT-TV. Today, there are 25 television stations in the state.

Mining coal

Mining

Mining produces only 2 percent of the state's gross product, but coal is the most valuable mineral resource. Most of the coal fields are in the north-central part of the state. The largest coal field is Warrior Field near Birmingham. Petroleum is found in the southwest region. The state leases thousands of acres offshore for oil and gas production.

Alabama established the first state-owned educational television system in the United States. The station went on the air in 1955. Today, the Alabama Public Television Network has nine stations in cities throughout the state and broadcasts to every county. The production arm of Alabama Public Television is the Center for Public Television and Radio (CPT&R) located in the College of Communications at the University of Alabama in Tuscaloosa. Along with programming of national importance, CPT&R produces the award-winning *The Alabama Experience,* which is broadcast from October through May. This series of programs focuses on the history and culture of the state. ■

Marble is another of valuable resource. The quality of Alabama's marble rivals or betters the famed marble of Italy. The state's high-quality marble is mined from the Piedmont Plateau. The Birmingham/Bessemer area depends on the state's huge seam of hematite (red iron ore) for its iron and steel production.

A steel-manufacturing plant

Manufacturing

The best-known manufacturing operations in Alabama are the iron- and steel-making industries located in the triangle area formed by Birmingham, Decatur, and Gadsden in the northern part of the state. One of the most awesome sights in Alabama is to watch raw ore being turned into the materials that make the roads, rails, skyscrapers, and trucks that help drive the country's economy.

Though Alabama is known for its metal manufacture, paper and pulp products are the state's leading manufactured goods. Paper, cardboard, paper bags, tissue, and other paper products are made at mills located in Mobile, Montgomery, and Childersburg.

Chemical production ranks second among Alabama's manufactured products. The chemicals produced in the state include industrial chemicals, chemical fibers (such as rayon), fertilizers, and insecticides. The leading chemical-producing cities are Decatur in the north and Mobile in the south.

Textiles are third in importance in the state's manufacturing. Alabama is among the leading textile-producers in the United States. Textile products, such as fabric, thread, and yarn, are produced throughout the state.

Primary-metal manufacturing, such as Bessemer's steel, ranks fourth in the state's manufactured products. Other items are machinery, rubber and plastic products, food products, and clothing. Manufacturing accounts for 22 percent of the gross state product and contributes more than $18 billion to Alabama's economy.

Fishing

Although it is only a small percentage of the gross state product, fishing is a $40-million-a-year industry. Alabama has both freshwater and saltwater commercial fishing. Most of the annual catch is taken from salt water. Shrimp is the biggest and most important catch. Other saltwater products include oysters, blue crabs, and red

Sloss Furnaces
The Sloss Furnace Company was founded in 1881 by Alabamian James Withers Sloss. Now designated a national historic landmark, this once-busy ironworks is featured on a walk-through museum of Birmingham's industrial past. There are exhibits on the method and process of turning coal, limestone, and ore into metal. Sloss was a working furnace until 1971.

Commercial fishing is done in both saltwater and freshwater locations.

snapper. The state's freshwater products are buffalo fish, catfish, and mussels. Catfish farming is new to the state, although Alabama ranks second in the country in its sales of catfish. The fish are raised in artificial ponds on farms and fed a grain diet.

Tourism

Alabama benefits from a multimillion-dollar tourist industry. Two of the state's leading attractions, Mardi Gras and the Azalea Trail Festival, are in Mobile. Birmingham hosts the Dogwood Festival, the annual Arts Festival, and the state fair. Auto-racing fans flock

U.S. Space and Rocket Center

Visitors to the U.S. Space and Rocket Center in Huntsville walk among rockets, spaceships, shuttles, lunar landing vehicles, and moon rocks. The Space Shot is a heart-stopping 4-G ride up a 180-foot (55-m) tower to experience two to three seconds of weightlessness.

At the Spacedome IMAX Theater, feature motion pictures are projected on a 67-foot (21-m) sur-round screen. A guided bus tour takes visitors to selected sites at the nearby Marshall Space Flight Center.

For the ultimate visit, sign up for Space Camp. It's not just for kids. This three-day weekend experience features astronaut-training activities, including lessons in what astronauts do in space and a simulated space-shuttle mission. ■

Free Enterprise Zones

One way Alabama attracts new businesses and industries to the state is by establishing areas called Free Enterprise Zones. Free Enterprise Zones offer state and local tax breaks and other incentives to encourage businesses to open headquarters or branch locations within Alabama. Alabama has Free Enterprise Zones in twenty-seven areas of the state—primarily in those places that need an economic boost. ■

to Alabama International Motor Speedway at Talladega. Special-collection libraries, state and national parks, and historical sites also bring eager tourists to the state.

Getting Wired

Most businesses and manufacturers within Alabama use computers to produce their products and services. More and more of these organizations are hooking up to the Internet as a way of increasing their sales and expanding their operations. This trend has created an entirely new and growing service industry that is beginning to have a major impact on the state's economy. Throughout Alabama, Internet providers, web masters, Internet directory services, and website consultants and designers are helping everyone "get wired." These providers serve big businesses, large manufacturers, small companies, and even home-based operations.

In 1989, the Alabama Supercomputer Authority (ASA) was established to develop the state's information highway through the Alabama Supercomputer Center (ASC). Its supercomputer is a

Many professionals rely on computer websites for the latest information.

Cray C94A, which provides high-tech and high-speed Internet connections and communications.

Business and industry use the ASC for product research. The ASC provides super speed and resources to Alabama's academic and industrial researchers to aid them in their advanced studies in science and engineering. ASC connects government, industry, and schools to the Internet. The supercomputer even carries interactive classroom instruction over its network. The ASC is located in Cumming Research Park near the Marshall Space Flight Center.

CHAPTER NINE

Sweet Home

The lyrics from the popular rock tune "Sweet Home Alabama" by Lynyrd Skynyrd express the virtues of life in Alabama. According to a U.S. census, 4,062,608 people were calling Alabama home in 1990. The estimated population in 1996 was 4,273,084. The state ranks twenty-second among the states in population.

The population density of Alabama is 79 people per square mile (30 people per square kilometer). The national average is 69 people per square mile (27 per square kilometer). Although Alabama had a rural population throughout most of its history, today two-thirds of the people live in urban areas. The state's six largest cities have populations that range from 54,000 to 266,000.

Ethnic Heritage

People born in Alabama tend to stay there. More than 3 million of the residents are natives of the state. Fewer than 45,000 of them were born outside of the United States.

A large portion of the population is of European ancestry: French, Spanish, English, Scottish, Irish, German, and Italian. The earliest settlers were the French and Spanish in the sixteenth through eighteenth centuries. In the mid-1880s, Scots, Irish, Germans, and Italians arrived to work the coal mines and iron furnaces around Birmingham. Across the bay in Baldwin County, Scandinavians, Italians, and Greeks settled in the late 1880s and early 1900s.

One-fourth of the population is of African descent. The first slaves were brought from Africa to Mobile in 1719. The black pop-

A Native American of Creek ancestry

Opposite: Senior citizens enjoying square dancing

Population of Alabama's Major Cities (1990)

Birmingham	265,968
Mobile	196,278
Montgomery	187,106
Huntsville	159,789
Tuscaloosa	77,759
Dothan	53,589

African-American youth must work hard to overcome the social and educational inequalities of the past.

ulation grew until it almost equaled the white population by 1816. From the Civil War until the 1970s, the African-American population in Alabama declined. In the late 1980s, that trend began to reverse. With social conditions greatly improved, many African-Americans are returning to their home state.

The Founding of Cullman

In 1866, Colonel John Cullmann fled to America from Germany's Landau region, which was then controlled by Russia. The colonel dreamed of creating a community for German immigrants. In 1873, he founded a colony in north-central Alabama and brought five families from Germany to establish farms and businesses. The growth and success of the settlement was so great that the state legislature recognized it as a county in 1877. In 1878, a town was incorporated and named after Colonel Cullmann. Seven years after the town of Cullman was founded, approximately 6,300 people resided in Cullman County. Today, the county's population is about 73,000. The town's population is almost 20,000.

The Cullman Chamber of Commerce and County Museum is housed in a replica of Colonel Cullmann's home. A 15-foot (4.6-m) bronze statue of the colonel stands facing city hall in the center of the city. Sculpted by Branko Medenica, the statue represents a cooperative effort between the city of Cullman and its sister city, Frankweiler, Germany, where Colonel Cullmann was born. ∎

The newest immigrants to the state are from Asia. At least 21,800 Asian refugees have settled in Alabama: Laotians in Opelika; Vietnamese in Bayou la Batre; and Cambodians in Irvington. Recently, people from China have settled in Montgomery. Native Americans make up only a small percentage of the population—16,500 as of the 1990 census.

Most Alabamians speak English. There are more than twenty-five languages spoken in the state, including most European languages. Other languages are Slavic, Scandinavian, Germanic, Indo-European, Arabic, the major Asian languages, and several Creole languages. Less than 3 percent of the population does not speak English.

Education

Education has been important to Alabamians from the earliest days of statehood. Alabama University was incorporated by the legislature in 1821. Construction on the tract of land in Tuscaloosa began in 1827, and classes began in 1831. Today, Alabama has twenty-seven colleges and universities that grant bachelor's and advanced degrees. These institutions

Alabama's population density

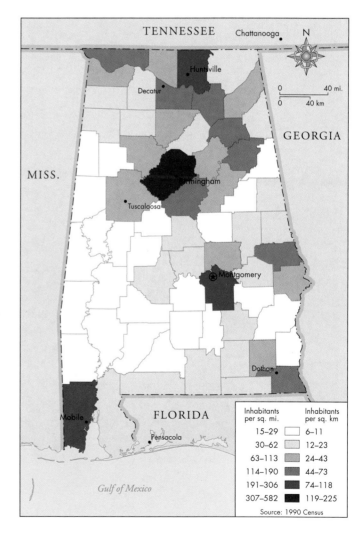

Inhabitants per sq. mi.		Inhabitants per sq. km
15–29		6–11
30–62		12–23
63–113		24–43
114–190		44–73
191–306		74–118
307–582		119–225

Source: 1990 Census

The mansion of the
president of Alabama
University

are accredited by the Southern Association of Colleges and Schools.

The state school system was established in 1854. Today, Alabama operates about 130 public school systems. Alabama law requires that all children from ages seven through fifteen attend school.

As part of the Department of Education's Trade and Industrial Education Service, there are eleven trade schools. Through these schools, businesses receive help training members of their workforce. Workers are paid trainees' wages while they attend the schools to learn specific jobs. This cooperative program is part of the incentive package that the state offers to attract new business and industry to the state.

There are private schools, junior colleges, technical institutes, and universities through-

Alabama's children now reap the benefits of totally integrated schools.

out Alabama. Some schools are operated by religious organizations, nonprofit groups, and individuals. The U.S. government runs the Community College of the Air Force at Maxwell Air Force base in Montgomery.

Single-family homes in the historic Oakleigh Garden District in Mobile

Living It Up in Alabama

Alabama offers many opportunities for people living diverse lifestyles. Life is fast paced and politically active in Montgomery. In Mobile, there is a high-fashion, trendy scene. In Birmingham, life moves to the beat of high finance and the arts. A high-tech crowd lives in the Huntsville area. For those looking for a slower pace, the small towns offer fishing, spelunking, annual festivals, and beach crawling.

The foods of Alabama are just as diverse as the ways of life. In Mobile, the diversity reflects the city's history. French and Spanish cuisine competes with Creole and Old South recipes to tempt residents and tourists alike. Restaurants and bakeries in several areas of the state serve authentic German food. Birmingham offers Italian and Greek cuisines. Home-style southern cooking can be found throughout the state. A fried-chicken dinner with all the trimmings is Alabama's definitive down-home meal.

Some Alabamians still maintain the southern hospitality and traditions of their ancestors.

Museums and Libraries

Most Alabamians live within driving distance of a museum. The state's many museums are devoted to everything from history to rock 'n' roll. There are

William Crawford Gorgas

Physician William Gorgas (1854–1920), a native of Toulminville, was one of the world's leading experts on public health. Among his many achievements was his work to control yellow fever and malaria. In 1900, while Gorgas was working in Havana, Cuba, there was an epidemic of yellow fever. When it was discovered that the disease was carried by mosquitoes, Gorgas ordered the elimination of mosquito-breeding places, which also eliminated the spread of the disease.

Gorgas also helped make possible the construction of the Panama Canal by destroying the disease-carrying mosquitoes there. In 1928, a government hospital near the city of Panama was named for him. In 1914, he became surgeon general of the U.S. Army.

The Gorgas Library, located on the campus of the University of Alabama honors Gorgas, his father, and his mother. His father, Confederate general Josiah Gorgas, was president of the university in 1887. His mother, Amelia, daughter of Governor John Gayle, was the university's nurse and librarian from 1883 until 1907. ■

Cahaba Hots

The woman who created this recipe says her family has always teased her about her thick southern accent. She lives in a part of Birmingham called Cahaba Heights. Because of her southern accent, she pronounces the word *heights* as *hots*—which is how this spicy recipe got its name.

Ingredients:

    4 cans of Vienna sausages
    1/4 cup of Demitri's Sauce
    1/4 cup of Durkee's Sauce
    dash of Louisiana Hot Sauce

Directions:

Grill the sausages. Combine and heat the remaining ingredients. Pour the sauce over the sausages. Serve them with toothpicks.

Serves eight to ten.

also art and natural-history museums. Military museums include the U.S. Army Aviation Museum, the space museum at Huntsville, and the Women's Army Corps Museum at Fort McClellan. The Aviation Museum at Fort Rucker is ranked as one of the largest such museums in the world. The museum at Fort McClellan is the only one dedicated to women in the armed services. The state also has many medical museums and medical libraries.

Public, university, law, history, literature, and special collections libraries are also found throughout the state. In 1901, Alabama created the Department of Archives and History, the first state-supported archives in the United States. Internet access to the archives is available through the Alabama Supercomputer network.

CHAPTER TEN

Sports and the Arts

A labamians are sports lovers. The state is full of fans, fanatics, and participants. There are no professional sports franchises in Alabama, but the state is home to many exciting teams and enthusiastic audiences.

Alabama's arts scene is also thriving—from folk dance to modern painting, classical music to popular song. The performing and visual arts are enjoyed, supported, and preserved throughout the state. The Alabama Arts Council encourages the arts through grants it receives from the National Endowment for the Arts and the state legislature. The council's Alabama Folk Life Program, for example, works to preserve traditional folk arts and to encourage artists to teach others.

Young Alabama sports fans

Fantastic Football

Mention Alabama sports, and the first thing people think of is the Crimson Tide. Well, for Auburn fans, it would probably be the second thing. The Crimson Tide and the Auburn Tigers have been competitors since the schools began playing team sports.

The Crimson Tide is the University of Alabama's football team. The Auburn Tigers play for Auburn University. Their fierce rivalry is settled every year after regular college-season play. The intrastate game, known as the Iron Bowl, determines the bragging rights for the rest of the year—regardless of which school won

Opposite: Following in the footsteps of an age-old tradition

Paul "Bear" Bryant

Paul "Bear" Bryant, born in Kingsland, Arkansas, is considered one of America's greatest college-football coaches. He earned his nickname by wrestling a bear. He played football in high school and at the University of Alabama, where he also had his first assistant-coaching job. As head coach, he led college teams at Maryland and Kentucky and coached the Texas Aggies for ten years.

Bryant returned to the University of Alabama in 1958. He coached several Crimson Tide football teams to 323 victories and 6 national championship titles. Under his leadership, the Alabama team was invited to the most post-season bowl games of any team in the league.

Bryant retired from the University of Alabama in 1982. He died in 1983. ■

which bowl or title. Between 1958 and 1982, the Crimson Tide, coached by Paul "Bear" Bryant, was able to do a lot of bragging.

The Tide/Tiger contest is not the only well-known football game in the state. The college all-star Blue-Gray Classic is played in Montgomery on Christmas Day. When they play in the Senior Bowl held in Mobile, college seniors from around the United States have their last audition for pro scouts. Pro football scouts have found a lot of talent in Alabama. The list includes linebacker Kevin Greene, receiver Bo Jackson, quarterback Ken Stabler, receiver John Stallworth, and quarterback Bart Starr.

Bo Jackson

Baseball Greats

There are three major-league baseball farm teams in the state. The Huntsville Stars (Oakland A's), Birmingham Barons (Chicago White Sox), and the Mobile BayBears (San Diego Padres) provide fans with the chance to see outstanding players—before they become rich and famous. The BayBears play in Hank Aaron Stadium, named in honor of the Mobile native who came to be known as Hammerin' Hank.

Some of the best-known names in baseball have gotten their start in Alabama. They include outfielders Bo Jackson, Willie Mays, and Willie McCovey, and pitchers Leroy "Satchel" Paige and Don Sutton.

In 1994, basketball superstar Michael Jordan tried to get his baseball start in Alabama, too—and the Birmingham Barons found themselves at the center of the sports universe. After retiring from the Chicago Bulls in 1993, Jordan decided to try playing pro baseball. Bulls owner Jerry Reinsdorf also owned the Chicago White Sox, and Jordan signed a minor-league contract to

Henry Louis "Hank" Aaron

Hank Aaron, born in Mobile in 1934, played professional baseball for twenty-one seasons. He finished his career with an all-time home-run record of 755, 2,297 RBIs (runs batted in), 3,000 hits, and 500 home runs. Known as Hammerin' Hank, his lifetime batting average was .310, with 3,771 hits. He was inducted into the Baseball Hall of Fame in 1982.

Baseball, however, is not Aaron's only accomplishment. Although a quiet, reserved man, he spoke out against the prejudice that he believed existed in professional baseball. He believed African-Americans were barred from coaching and administrative positions. For his efforts, the National Association for the Advancement of Colored People (NAACP) awarded him its highest award, the Spingarn Medal, in 1974. ∎

The Alabama Sports Hall of Fame

Established in Birmingham in 1967, the Alabama Sports Hall of Fame preserves and honors the state's long sports heritage. The exhibits document the lives and careers of great athletes who have excelled in a wide range of sports. Some of the many athletes memorialized there are Jesse Owens (track), Joe Lewis (boxing), Joe Namath (football), Bobby and Davey Allison (racing), and Jennifer Chandler Jones (diving). ■

play with the Sox's AA affiliate, Birmingham. Despite the fact that Jordan didn't play very well—he hit just .202 in 127 games—the Barons set attendance records that season at home and on the road. Jordan rejoined the Bulls and led them to several more championships.

Tracks and Links

Talladega Superspeedway east of Birmingham is a 2.66-mile (4.3-km) tri-oval raceway. Professional race-car drivers round the track at average speeds of nearly 190 miles (306 km) per hour. The Winston 500 and the Sears DieHard 500 run on this track. Birmingham, Mobile, and Shorter have greyhound-racing tracks with simulcasted horse races.

Golf fans trek to Alabama to play the Robert Trent Jones Golf Trail. The trail includes eighteen championship courses in seven locations throughout the state, offering 324 holes and 100 miles (161 km) of golfing. The trail was designed by and named for famed golf-course architect Robert Trent Jones Sr. Jones has

James Cleveland Owens

Olympic track star Jesse Owens was born in Oakville in 1913. When he was young, his family called him J. C.—short for James Cleveland. The family moved to Ohio when James was nine years old. When his new teacher asked his name, she misunderstood his answer and entered Jesse instead of J. C. The name stuck.

Owens began his athletic career in 1928, setting new world records while he was a junior in high school. At the 1936 Berlin Olympic Games, Owens won three gold medals. After the Olympics, Owens dedicated his life to working with disadvantaged youth. President Gerald Ford presented Owens with the Medal of Freedom in 1976. President Jimmy Carter presented him with the Living Legend Award in 1979. Owens died on March 31, 1980. ■

designed more than 500 golf courses around the world, and 35 of them are among the top 100 courses in America.

The Sounds of Alabama

Alabama is a major center for traditional American music. The state's musicians are nationally known artists of jazz, blues, gospel, country, and rock. These uniquely American music styles are featured in festivals and museums throughout the state. The music plays on during the W. C. Handy Music Festival in Florence and the Tennessee Valley Old Time Fiddlers Convention at Athens State College. Music legends are preserved in the Alabama Jazz Hall of Fame, the Alabama Music Hall of Fame and Museum, and the

Talented musicians keep Alabama's musical traditions alive.

ALABAMA Fan Club and Museum in Fort Payne, which spotlights the country-music group ALABAMA.

Among the many famous musicians and musical groups from Alabama are Brother Cane (a rock and blues band), Bibi Black (classical trumpet player), Jimmy Buffet (pop singer), The Commodores (Motown pop group), Nat "King" Cole (singer and piano player), Cleveland Eaton (jazz musician), Sonny James (country singer), Lionel Richie (pop singer), Percy Sledge (soul singer), Take 6 (contemporary Christian group), and Tammy Wynette (country singer).

Lionel Richie

Tammy Wynette

Classical music is also on the scene in Alabama. The Alabama Symphony Orchestra in Birmingham and the Huntsville Symphony Orchestra offer full seasons of concerts of classic and popular music. Montgomery has a volunteer orchestra that presents a five-concert classics series and gives free pop concerts throughout the city. Every April, Guntersville offers the Gerhart Chamber Music Festival. Chamber groups and world-renowned musicians perform traditional and contemporary music throughout Marshall County. Operas are performed in Huntsville, Fort Payne, and Mobile. Mobile's opera company, founded in 1946, offers children's matinees called Opera a-la-Carte and an in-school program, Kids Creating Opera, which introduces young people to this art form.

Two Music Legends

Musician and composer William Christopher "W. C." Handy (above left), born in Florence in 1873, is called the Father of the Blues. While he was attending public school, an influential music teacher provided him with solid training. Handy sang and played trumpet and cornet. As he began to write music, he developed a unique style that would later be known as "the blues." In 1912, he published "Memphis Blues," the first tune with the word *blues* in the title. In 1914, he wrote "St. Louis Blues" and "Yellow Dog Blues."

In 1918, Handy opened a music-publishing firm in New York City. An eye disease was causing his sight to deteriorate, however, and Handy was blind by 1923. He stopped performing but continued to work with orchestras. In his lifetime, Handy wrote more than 150 musical compositions. Many parks, streets, statues, museums, and festivals bear his name. The most prestigious honor a blues artist can receive is the W. C. Handy Award.

Another Alabama son, Hiram "Hank" Williams (above right), is known as the Father of Modern Country Music. Born in Georgiana in 1923, Williams was a superstar by the age of twenty-five. Unlike most country singers of his time, he wrote his own music, developing his own distinctive sound. He would croon his songs sweetly or growl them in a honky-tonk style—the audiences loved them all. His success did not carry over into his personal life, however. After his first marriage failed, Williams began to abuse drugs and alcohol. He died in 1953 at the age of twenty-nine.

In his brief career, Williams had eleven of his songs hit number one on the music charts. He won a Grammy Award in 1952. Thanks to the technology that allows digital remastering of old tapes, an album of duets sung by Williams and his son, Hank Williams Jr., won a Grammy in 1987. ■

Theater and Dance

The Alabama Shakespeare Festival is the fifth-largest Shakespeare festival in the world. Founded in Anniston in 1972, the festival moved to Montgomery in 1985 after Winton and Carolyn Blount funded the building of the performing arts complex there. Production organizations in Huntsville include Broadway Theatre League, Fantasy Playhouse, Independent Musical Productions, Lee Lyric Theatre, Theatre Huntsville, and Theatre 'Round the Corner. Professional and amateur theater is staged in civic centers, restored theaters and opera houses, and outdoor amphitheaters, such as Looney's Amphitheater in Winston County.

Each year, the Alabama Shakespeare Festival is held at the performing arts complex in Montgomery.

The Birmingham Children's Theatre (BCT), founded in 1947 by the Junior League, is now a professional company. One of the largest children's theaters in the United States, it presents more than 600 performances annually. The company operates three performance spaces in the Birmingham-Jefferson Civic Center. It also has a traveling company called Theatre in Motion. BCT's many series include programs for students from preschool through grades twelve, Family Performances, the Guest Artist Series, and the Holiday Series.

Alabama also has ballet companies, history reenactment productions, and arts festivals. Mobile hosts the Mardi Gras, a citywide performance event. Famous stage and screen performers from Alabama include Tallulah Bankhead (a film actor of the 1930s and 1940s), actor and comedian Brett Butler, actor Courtney Cox, actor George Lindsey, actor and singer Jim Nabors, and comedian Paula Poundstone.

Art and Architecture

There are exhibits and museums of fine arts in cities and towns throughout Alabama. The Birmingham Museum of Art is the home of a nationally recognized permanent collection of more than 17,000 works from ancient to modern times. The museum's Asian art collection is the largest in the Southeast. There are also collec-

The Alabama Artists Gallery in Montgomery

tions of Renaissance paintings, art of the American West, the largest collection of Wedgewood china outside of England, a collection of eighteenth-century French art, and the world's largest display of decorative cast iron.

The Montgomery Museum of Fine Arts houses American art by artists such as John Singer Sargent, Winslow Homer, and Georgia O'Keeffe. There is also a permanent collection of southern regional art.

To see Alabama's best collection of historic art and architecture under one roof, visit the state capitol. The oldest portion of the building, at the center of the structure, was built in 1851. This section was the first capitol of the Confederacy and is a national landmark. The 1851 building, designed in the Greek Revival style, has high ceilings and interior columns. The center dome displays eight large murals, 13 by 11 feet (4 by 3.4 m), that depict scenes from Alabama's history.

The murals under the capitol dome

Alabama's Writers

Alabama has an impressive list of writers, from novelists and journalists to romance and comedy writers. The state's literary talent can be found in libraries and bookstores throughout the country— as well as on the screen and stage. Some of Alabama's best-known

Restoring the Capitol

The capitol-restoration project began in 1986 and was completed in 1992. Artists used centuries-old techniques to recreate the panels, ceiling plasterwork, and frescoes that decorated the original structure, which was built in 1851. The supreme court chamber, which had been made into offices in the 1940s, was restored to its original size and again features two Corinthian columns.

The new north, south, and east wings were designed in neoclassic style, a revival of the architecture of ancient Greece and Rome. The columns in the 1992 addition to the east wing were cast from the original molds used for the 1851 west portico, where Jefferson Davis was inaugurated as president of the Confederate States of America. The rooms in the capital are decorated with original and reproduction furnishings. ■

writers are Fannie Flagg (*Fried Green Tomatoes at the Whistle Stop Cafe*), Winston Groom (*Forrest Gump*), and Dennis Covington (*Lasso the Moon*).

The most famous of all Alabama writers is a woman who wrote only one book. Nelle Harper Lee of Monroeville was born in 1926. During the years of her early childhood, the Scottsboro Boys trials were making the news. The events formed the basis for Lee's only published novel, *To Kill a Mockingbird*. The book was awarded a Pulitzer Prize for fiction in 1961. The novel was made into an Academy Award–winning film and later into a stage play. A study conducted by the Library of Congress revealed that *To Kill a Mockingbird* is the second-most-influential book that American readers have experienced—first place went to the Bible. Lee's novel was first published in 1960 and has never been out of print.

Fannie Flagg

Against the backdrop of its natural beauty and its historical challenges and victories, Alabama has developed a unique spirit. The voices of these writers blend with the many other voices of the people of Alabama—business people, politicians, scientists, and workers. As they strive for personal accomplishments, these diverse people are working together to improve the future of their "sweet home."

Timeline

United States History

1607 The first permanent British settlement is established in North America at Jamestown.

1620 Pilgrims found Plymouth Colony, the second permanent British settlement.

1776 America declares its independence from England.

1783 The Treaty of Paris officially ends the Revolutionary War in America.

1787 The U.S. Constitution is written.

Alabama State History

1519 Spanish explorer Alonso Álvarez de Piñeda sails into Mobile Bay.

1540 Hernando de Soto explores much of the area that is now Alabama.

1559 Tristán de Luna establishes temporary settlement on Mobile Bay.

1702 French settlers led by Sieur d'Iberville and Sieur de Bienville found Fort Louis de la Mobile on the Mobile River.

1763 The Treaty of Paris ends the French and Indian War, and France gives the lands that make up present-day Alabama to Great Britain.

1780 Spain captures Mobile from the British.

1783 Britain cedes northern Alabama to the United States and the Mobile region to Spain.

United States History

The Louisiana Purchase almost **1803** doubles the size of the United States.

U.S and Britain **1812–15** fight the War of 1812.

The North and South fight each **1861–65** other in the American Civil War.

The United States is **1917–18** involved in World War I.

The stock market crashes, **1929** plunging the United States into the Great Depression.

The United States fights in **1941–45** World War II.

The United States becomes a **1945** charter member of the United Nations.

The United States fights **1951–53** in the Korean War.

The U.S. Congress enacts a series of **1964** groundbreaking civil rights laws.

The United States **1964–73** engages in the Vietnam War.

The United States and other **1991** nations fight the brief Persian Gulf War against Iraq.

Alabama State History

1817 Congress organizes the Alabama Territory.

1819 Alabama becomes the twenty-second state on December 14.

1846 Montgomery becomes the state capital.

1861 Alabama secedes from the United States and briefly becomes the Republic of Alabama before joining the Confederacy.

1868 Alabama is readmitted to the United States.

1901 Current state constitution is adopted.

1931–37 The Scottsboro Boys trials lead to historic decisions by the Supreme Court.

1946 Work begins on the Tennessee-Tombigbee Waterway.

1955 Rosa Parks's refusal to give up her seat on a Montgomery bus leads to a year-long bus boycott.

1965 Martin Luther King Jr. leads thousands on a march from Selma to Montgomery to protest voter discrimination. The march leads to the passage of the Voting Rights Act of 1965.

1982 George C. Wallace becomes the first Alabama governor to be elected to a fourth term.

1993 Rosa Parks is inducted into National Women's Hall of Fame.

Fast Facts

The capitol

Statehood date	December 14, 1819, the 22nd state
Origin of state name	From the American Indian tribe of the same name, meaning "I open [clear] the thicket"
State capital	Montgomery
State nicknames	Heart of Dixie, Cotton State, Yellowhammer State
State motto	*Audemus Jura Nostra Defendere* (We Dare Defend Our Rights)
State bird	Yellowhammer
State flower	Camellia
State saltwater fish	Tarpon
State freshwater fish	Largemouth bass
State mineral	Hematite (red iron ore)
State rock	Marble
State horse	Racking horse
State game bird	Wild turkey
State American folk dance	Square dance

Camellia

A pecan grove

State nut	Pecan
State fossil	*Basilosaurus cetoides*
State insect	Monarch butterfly
State reptile	Red-bellied turtle
State gemstone	Star blue quartz
State song	"Alabama"
State tree	Southern longleaf pine
State reptile	Red-bellied turtle
State fair	Birmingham (early October)
Total area; rank	52,237 sq. mi. (135,294 sq km); 30th
Land; rank	50,750 sq. mi. (131,444 sq km); 28th
Water; rank	1,487 sq. mi. (3,851 sq km); 20th
***Inland water;* rank**	968 sq. mi. (2,507 sq km); 23rd
***Coastal water;* rank**	519 sq. mi. (1,344 sq km); 12th
Geographic center	Chilton, 12 miles (19 km) southwest of Clanton
Latitude and longitude	Alabama is located approximately between 84° 51'and 88° 28' N and 30° 13' and 35° 00' W
Highest point	Cheaha Mountain, 2,407 feet (734 m)
Lowest point	Sea level along the Gulf of Mexico
Largest city	Birmingham
Number of counties	67

At Mount Cheaha
State Park

Some of Alabama's youth

Population; rank	4,062,608 (1990 census); 22nd
Density	79 persons per sq. mi. (30 per sq km)
Population distribution	89% urban, 11% rural

Ethnic distribution (does not equal 100%)		
	White	73.65%
	African-American	25.26%
	Hispanic	0.61%
	Asian and Pacific Islanders	0.54%
	Other	0.19%
	Native American	0.41%

Record high temperature	112°F (44°C) at Centreville on September 5, 1925
Record low temperature	–27°F (–33°C) at New Market on January 30, 1966
Average July temperature	80°F (27°C)
Average January temperature	46°F (8°C)
Average annual precipitation	56 inches (142 cm)

Natural Areas and Historic Sites

National Military Park

Horseshoe Bend National Military Park is the site of the 1814 defeat of the Creek Nation.

National Historic Site

Tuskegee Institute National Historic Site is the site of the black college founded by Booker T. Washington.

National Parkway

Natchez Trace Parkway National Scenic Trail follows the historic route used by Native Americans and early settlers from Natchez, Mississippi, through Alabama, to Nashville, Tennessee.

National Scenic Trail

Natchez Trace National Scenic Trail includes segments of the 694-mile (1,117-km) scenic trail that lies alongside the Natchez Trace Parkway.

National Monument

Russell Cave National Monument contains the archaeological record of nearly 9,000 years of human habitation.

National Preserve

Little River Canyon National Preserve is a unique environment for threatened and endangered species.

State Parks

Blue Springs State Park visitors can swim in a pool fed by underground spring water.

DeSoto State Park contains one of the deepest canyons east of the Mississippi River.

Gulf State Park has white sand beaches and a long fishing pier on the Gulf of Mexico.

Monte Sano State Park includes Natural Well, a huge circular hole whose depth is still unknown.

Oak Mountain State Park is the largest state park in Alabama.

Russell Cave

Sports Teams

NCAA Teams (Division 1)

Alabama State University Hornets

Auburn University Tigers

Jacksonville State University Gamecocks

Samford University Bulldogs

Troy State University Trojans

University of Alabama Crimson Tide

University of Alabama-Birmingham Blazers

University of South Alabama Jaguars

Cultural Institutions

Libraries

Amelia Gayle Gorgas Library at the University of Alabama (Mobile) houses an outstanding collection of reference material on the history and culture of Alabama.

The Department of Archives and History is the first state-supported archives in the U.S. and contains a wealth of information on Alabama's history.

Museums

Birmingham Museum of Art

Montgomery Museum of Fine Arts

Berman Museum (Anniston) has a collection of 1,500 weapons that once belonged to people ranging from Napoléon I to Jefferson Davis.

The Birmingham Civil Rights Museum has exhibits depicting the struggles for civil rights, including the racial segregation of the 1920s and achievements made up to the present day.

The capitol dome

Performing Arts

Alabama has two symphony orchestras, one major opera company, one major dance company, and one major professional theater company.

Universities and Colleges

In the mid-1990s, Alabama had fifteen public and twelve private institutions of higher learning.

Annual Events

Mardi Gras

Peach orchard

January–March

Mardi Gras in Mobile (February–March)

Azalea Spectacular in Mobile (February–March)

Zoo Weekend in Montgomery (March)

Selma Pilgrimage Weekend (March)

April–June

Eufaula Pilgrimage (April)

Birmingham Festival of Arts (April)

Birmingham Rose Show (May)

Panoply, a festival of the visual and performing arts, in Huntsville (May)

City Stages in Birmingham (June)

Chilton County Peach Festival in Clanton (June)

America's Junior Miss in Mobile (late June)

July–September

DieHard 500 in Talladega (July)

W. C. Handy Music Festival in Florence (early August)

River Boat Regatta in Guntersville (August)

October–December

South Alabama State Fair in Montgomery (October)

National Shrimp Festival in Gulf Shores (October)

National Peanut Festival in Dothan (November)

Annual Thanksgiving Day Pow Wow in Atmore (November)

Blue-Gray Football Game in Montgomery (December)

Famous People

Henry "Hank" Aaron

Martin Luther King Jr.

Henry "Hank" Aaron (1934–)	Baseball player
John Hollis Bankhead (1842–1920)	U.S. senator
Tallulah Brockman Bankhead (1903–1968)	Actress
Hugo LaFayette Black (1886–1971)	U.S. Supreme Court associate justice
Paul "Bear" Bryant (1913–1983)	Football coach
George Washington Carver (1864–1943)	Botanist and educator
Nathaniel Adams "Nat King" Cole (1919–1965)	Popular singer
William Christopher Handy (1873–1958)	Musician and composer
John William Heisman (1869–1936)	Football coach
Helen Adams Keller (1880–1968)	Author and lecturer
Coretta Scott King (1927–)	Civil rights leader
Martin Luther King Jr. (1929–1968)	Minister and civil rights leader
Nelle Harper Lee (1926–)	Author
Joe Louis (1914–1981)	Boxer

George Wallace

Willie Howard Mays Jr. (1931–)	Baseball player
Alexander McGillivray (1759?–1793)	Indian leader
James Cleveland (Jesse) Owens (1913–1980)	Athlete
Rosa Parks (1913–)	Civil rights leader
Tuscaloosa	Choctaw leader
George Corley Wallace (1919–1998)	Alabama governor
Booker Taliaferro Washington (1856–1915)	Lecturer, author, and educator
Dinah Washington (1924–1967)	Jazz and blues singer and piano player
Hiram "Hank" Williams (1923–1953)	Country and western singer

To Find Out More

History

- Brown, Dottie. *Alabama*. Minneapolis: Lerner, 1994.

- Fradin, Dennis Brindell. *Alabama*. Chicago: Childrens Press, 1993

- Hahn, Elizabeth. *The Creek.* Vero Beach, Fla.: Rourke, 1992.

- Perdue, Theda. *The Cherokee*. New York: Chelsea House, 1989.

- Reger, James P. *Life in the South During the Civil War*. San Diego: Lucent Books, 1997.

- Stein, R. Conrad. *The Montgomery Bus Boycott*. Chicago: Childrens Press, 1993

- Stein, R. Conrad. *The Story of the Trail of Tears*. Chicago: Childrens Press, 1985.

- Thompson, Kathleen. *Alabama*. Austin, Tex.: Raintree Publications; 1988.

- Wills, Charles A. *A Historical Album of Alabama*. Brookfield, Conn.: Millbrook Press, 1995.

Fiction

- Johnson, Angela. *The Other Side: Shorter Poems*. New York: Orchard Books, 1998.

- McKissack, Patricia C. *Run Away Home*. New York: Scholastic, 1997.

Biographies

- Christman, Abbott, and Rick Whipple. *Hernando De Soto*. Austin, Tex.: Raintree/Steck-Vaughn, 1996.

- Hull, Mary. *Rosa Parks*. New York: Chelsea House, 1994.
- Nicholson, Lois P., et al. *George Washington Carver*. Broomall, Penn.: Chelsea House, 1994.
- Parks, Rosa, with Jim Haskins. *Rosa Parks: My Story*. New York: Dial Books, 1992.

Websites

- **Alabama State Website**

  http://www.state.al.us/general/

  Information on Alabama's history and government

- **Alabama Live**

  http://www.al.com/south/

  Site includes information on colleges, parks, statewide calendar of events, people, food, and folk legends

- **University of Alabama Center for Public Television and Radio**

  http://www.cptr.ua.edu

Links to statewide television and radio programming.

- **Montgomery Home Page**

  http://www.montgomery-al.com/

  Everything you want to know about Montgomery

- **Fort Morgan**

  http://www2.msstate.edu/~acb9/coastal.html

  Picture and text tour of Fort Morgan

Addresses

- **Office of the Secretary of State**

  State Capitol

  Montgomery, AL 36130

  For information on Alabama's government

- **Alabama Tourism and Travel**

  PO Box 4927

  401 Adams Avenue

  Montgomery, AL 36103

  For information on travel and tourism in Alabama

Index

Page numbers in *italics* indicate illustrations.

Meet the Author

Lucile Davis is a native Texan and lives in Fort Worth. She is the author of a number of books for young people about interesting places and people. Her most recent title for Children's Press is *The Mayo Brothers* for the Community Builders series. She holds a bachelor's degree in English from the University of Missouri at St. Louis and a master's degree in theater from Texas Christian University.

Davis did the research for this book mainly through the library, the telephone, and the Internet. She says the people of Alabama "bent over backward" to help her. They researched, copied, made phone calls, and mailed dozens of envelopes full of material.

Some of the best Internet sites for her research were the Alabama State site, Alabama Live, and the University of Alabama Center for Public Television and Radio. One of the most important

books that she consulted for this research was *Alabama Off the Beaten Path: A Guide to Unique Places* by Gay Martin. The book is just what it says it is—and more. Davis says that if you are planning to visit Alabama, this is the tour-guide book to have along with you.

Photo Credits

Photographs ©:

Alabama Bureau of Tourism and Travel: 7 top right, 12, 13, 20, 71 right, 121

AP/Wide World Photos: 73, 133 top (Kiichiro Sato)

Aristock, Inc.: 74 (Peter Beney), 6 top right, 62 (Robb Helfrick), 124 (Jean Higgins), 7 top left, 59, 60 (Roger Idenden), 9, 47, 71 left, 72, 79 top, 108 (Andre Jenny), 85, 129 top (Rod Kaye), 89, 133 (Ken Krakow), 101 (Bill Lai), 8 (William Schemmel)

Audrey Gibson: 45

Black Star/PNI: 76, 135 (Vernon Merritt)

Bud Hunter: 52, 54, 57, 93, 94, 102, 107, 113, 123, 129 bottom, 132

Corbis-Bettmann: 6 top left, 37, 42, 44, 46, 48, 79 bottom, 80, 114, 134 bottom (UPI), 22, 28, 33, 117, 120 left

David J. Forbert: cover, 68

David R. Frazier: 69, 103

Envision: 111 (Osentoski & Zoda)

Gamma-Liaison, Inc.: 122 (Carl Bergquist), 90 (Ed Lallo), 6 bottom, 24 (Schwarz), 92 (Alan Weiner)

Globe Photos: 125 (Ralph Dominguez), 119 bottom (Alpha/Paul Harris), 115, 120 right, 134 top

H. Armstrong Roberts, Inc.: 14, 131 (George Hunter), back cover (W. Metzen)

Mark E. Gibson: 51, 99, 104, 130

National Geographic Image Collection: 112, 118 (Dick Durrance), 37 (Bates Littlehales), 7 bottom, 43 (Richard T. Nowitz), 109 (Joseph J. Scherschel), 65 (John Schneeberger)

North Wind Picture Archives: 7 top center, 55 (N. Carter), 17, 25, 27, 29, 39

Photo Researchers: 38 (Degginger), 87 right (Bruce Roberts)

Stock Boston: 53 (William Johnson)

Stock Montage, Inc.: 30, 31, 34, 83

Superstock, Inc.: 61, 75, 82, 84, 128 bottom

Sygma: 119 top (Michael Jacobs)

Tony Stone Images: 95 (Bruce Ando), 15 left (Raymond Barnes), 15 right, 16 (Richard A. Cooke III), 88 (David James), 2 (James Randklev), 36 (Andy Sacks), 64 (Mark Segal), 6 top center, 98 (Vince Streano), 96 (Keith Wood)

University of Alabama: 106 (Alice Wilson), 110

Visuals Unlimited: 87 lcft (Scott Berner)

Maps by XNR Productions, Inc.